"Who's Who In Interior Design" Presents
100 DESIGNERS' FAVORITE ROOMS

John L. Pellam

Foreword by Michael de Santis

Barons Who's Who

SELECTED PROJECTS OF THE WORLD'S FINEST INTERIOR DESIGNERS
NORTH AMERICA • EUROPE • ASIA • SOUTH AMERICA

Page one: Joseph P. Horan (design), John Vaughan (photog.); *page two:* Sandra Nunnerley
(design), Feliciano (photog.); *title page:* Edward Turrentine (design),
Douglas Hill (photog.); *page four:* Michael de Santis (design), Phillip H. Ennis (photog.);
contents page: Ricardo Mayer (design), Juca Moraes (photog.);
page 224: Maureen Sullivan Stemberg (design), Peter Vitale (photog.).

Distributed worldwide by Baker + Taylor International
652 East Main Street, Bridgewater, New Jersey 08807
(908) 218-0400. Fax: (908) 707-4387

Published by Barons Who's Who
412 North Coast Highway, B-110, Laguna Beach, California 92651
(714) 497-8615. Fax: (714) 786-8918

10 9 8 7 6 5 4 3 2 1

Library of Congress Catalogue Number 92-74174
International Standard Book Number 1-882292-00-6

Typography by Typesetting & Graphics, Laguna Hills, California
Printed and bound in Hong Kong

CONTENTS

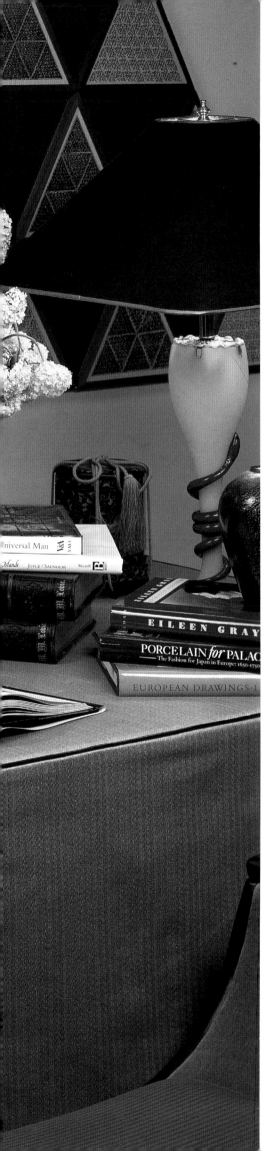

FOREWORD

*I*n your hands, you hold the choices made by one hundred interior designers when asked to pick a favorite room from all their creations. Each had personal reasons for making that one final selection. Perhaps there were one hundred different ways to make this choice. Surely the viewer may not agree with all the choices and will have personal favorites, but in each room you will find some element that pleases and inspires you.

*T*he tastes and cultural styles presented in this book illustrate the diversity of interior design currently being created throughout the world. Leading designers from Asia, Europe, North and South America and other parts of the globe have all contributed their favorite projects to this volume. All have selected what they feel is their best work, their finest design, their most unique interior concept, their favorite room.

*A*s one of the designers participating in this book, I know choosing my favorite room was no easy task. How does one select only a single design from among the myriad of rooms completed throughout a career? Does one go with the showcase room that allowed the most creative freedom, the least budget restriction, the most artistic *carte blanche*? Does one choose a room designed for a particularly favorite client? Perhaps the room that was easiest? Or considering how they'll be remembered, does one choose that room full of timeless objects and traditionally proven period pieces, a room that will immortalize them by always being historically 'correct'? In a sense, my favorite is always the room I'm currently working on, the visionary challenge of the moment. After all, the artist in us always hopes the next room will be better than any that came before it.

*W*hether the room is within a formal mansion or a casual seaside retreat, whether it is within a private residence or a corporate headquarters, it should be remembered that, at most times, designers do not have a completely free hand. They design environments for people to live in and work in, and, therefore, must compromise their imaginations to fit the requirements of the client. Thus, as you study the pictures presented to you on these pages, you should take into consideration the needs and tastes of the client as you gauge the performance of the designers.

*A*bove all, ask yourself one question: "are there enough elements I like about the room for me to seek out this particular designer?" Certainly, given the wide range of styles represented here, the answer will be yes, and you too can find your favorite choice.

Michael de Santis, ASID

---

*A classical wall design accents this library table
in the 1992 Kips Bay Boys' and Girls' Club Designer Showhouse.
Interior design: Sandra Nunnerley. Photography: Feliciano.*

INTRODUCTION

*T*his book is presented to you as an international portfolio of the finest work of the world's leading interior and architectural designers. One hundred designers are featured, each displaying their favorite design project.

*I*nherent in the very nature of this book is diversity in both style and geography. Thus, the following pages have been divided into four sections: North America East, North America West, International, and Worldwide Contract Design. The first three sections feature residential projects in their respective geographical areas, while the fourth presents commercial design projects from throughout the world. So that you may easily use this book to select your next interior designer, it is completed with a contact directory of all featured designers.

• • • • •

I'd like you to think of the following two hundred-plus pages as a world tour, taking you to exotic cities around the globe, and into the world's most beautifully designed homes, galleries, offices and hotels.

*Y*ou begin your tour with residential designs, where you'll see the interiors of homes, penthouses and estates throughout the major cities of North America. In the International section you'll journey from Paris to Rio de Janeiro, from Tokyo to Bermuda, from London to Bombay, and then on to Oslo, Montevideo and Kuala Lumpur, with stops in Paraguay, Ireland and the Middle East. Next you're off to see the world's finest hotels, offices, and commercial centers. You'll tour New York's Trump Tower, Claridge's in London, the Amanusa Resort Hotel in Bali, Jamaica's Grand Lido Hotel, China's exotic Garden Hotel Shanghai and Jakarta's Sahid Jaya Hotel, along with a tour of office designs in Europe, North and South America, India and Asia.

*A*s you travel the globe, you'll be introduced to one hundred of the world's most creative and talented designers – people on the cutting edge of international design. As you meet each designer, you'll see their finest work, listen as they explain why the room shown is their favorite, and learn what innovations they employed to overcome the challenges each room presented.

*W*hen your tour is completed, you'll have discovered an abundance of new design ideas. And if your journey has been successful, by the time you return to your own home you'll have at least one designer in mind for your next interior design project – a project that could easily become that designer's new favorite!

John L. Pellam

St. Florient marble, polished bronze, and bronze tinted glass create a dramatic entrance to New York's 505 Park Avenue Building. Interior design: Der Scutt, FAIA. Photography: Peter Mauss.

THE MAJOR DESIGN ASSOCIATIONS

*B*ecause many of the designers featured within this volume are members of one or more professional design associations, a brief explanation of the purposes and goals of a representative number of these organizations is offered upon the following pages. The American Institute of Architects (AIA), the American Society of Interior Designers (ASID), the Institute of Business Designers (IBD), and the International Society of Interior Designers (ISID) have each submitted the information on their respective organizations presented here.

*O*ther organizations of which featured designers are members include the Association of German Interior Architects (BDI), the Bermuda Society of Interior Designers (BSID), the Chartered Society of Designers (CSD), the Chinese Society of Interior Designers (CSID), the Hong Kong Institute of Architects (HKIA), the Indonesian Society of Interior Designers (HDII), the Interior Decorators & Designers Association (IDDA), the Interior Designers of New Brunswick (IDNB), the International Design & Furnishings Association (IDFA), the Jamaica Institute of Architects (JIA), the Japan Institute of Architects (JIA), the Japan Interior Designers' Association (JID), and the Norwegian Interior Architects Association (NIL). Professional status within an organization is indicated when the initials of the design organization follow a designer's name. Members achieving Professional status have fulfilled exacting education and experience requirements and, for a number of organizations, have passed a nationally administered examination testing a comprehensive range of design principles and standards. Fellow membership (e.g.: FASID) is an esteemed recognition granted to those designers whom have exhibited outstanding professional conduct, expertise and participation within their organizations.

*T*hese design organizations have set the highest standards of quality, service and competence for their members, and they provide and encourage continued education in all aspects of architectural and interior design. To this end, specific entities have been created to regulate and monitor the interior design profession. The National Council for Interior Design Qualification (NCIDQ) administers qualifying examinations, the passage of which are required by many organizations in order to receive a 'Professional' designation. The Foundation for Interior Design Education Research (FIDER) is governed by design practitioners and educators from the ASID, the Interior Design Educators Council, the IBD and the Interior Designers of Canada. This foundation handles special accreditation of interior design education offered at institutions of higher education throughout the United States and Canada.

A fanciful mood is created in this recreation room designed with neon, glass block wall, and sofa made from 50's-era automobile fenders. Interior design: Walter Nelson, ASID. Photography: Kim Brun.

The American Institute of Architects

Headquartered in Washington, D.C., The American Institute of Architects (AIA) is the preeminent professional association representing America's architects since 1957. More than 55,000 members adhere to a Code of Ethics and Professional Conduct that assures the client, the public, and colleagues of an architect's dedication to the highest standards in professional practice.

Through public outreach, education, and government affairs initiatives, the AIA works to serve its membership and the public at large. Community design and development initiatives encourage well-designed, affordable housing for all Americans. By forging coalitions of architects, community leaders, and representatives of other professional disciplines, the AIA works to create urban environments that are inviting, affirming expressions of community life. By speaking with a united voice, architects in the AIA can also influence government decisions that affect the practice of the profession and quality of American life. Together with its more than 300 state and local organizations, the Institute promotes public and professional betterment through legislative advocacies such as accessibility to all Americans and protection of the nation's neglected infrastructure.

The Institute serves its members with professional development opportunities, information services, personal benefits, and client-oriented resources. Contract documents developed and revised by the AIA are the model for the design and construction industry. And programs such as the Intern-Architect Development Program, registration-exam preparation courses, and employment referral services serve architecture students and future architects. AIA members also participate in volunteer professional committees specializing in such arenas as design, interiors, education, the environment, housing, regional and urban design, and historic resources. Among the broad range of AIA professional interest areas, the Interiors program establishes vital links with various services and approaches within the interiors community, and develops liaisons with manufacturers and custom-service providers on quality, cost, and environmental issues. The Institute also hosts a "Design Excellence in the Architecture of Interiors" initiative, to help interior architects recognize and embrace the linkage between competency, success, innovation, and excellence in view of increasing competition in a global marketplace.

Nationally recognized AIA awards programs set the standard for architectural excellence while cultivating an ever-growing audience for good design. The annual event, "Accent on Architecture," publicly celebrates design excellence, while the AIA Fellowship Program recognizes notable contributions of its members. In partnership with The American Architectural Foundation (AAF), the AIA strives for a national design literacy in the belief that a well-trained, creative profession and an informed public are prerequisites for an enhanced quality of American life.

*Reclad in five colors of marble, the lobby walls and floor of New York's
1633 Broadway Building reflect light shining from Art Deco-inspired fixtures.
Interior design by AIA member Der Scutt, photography by Roy Wright.*

The American Society of Interior Designers

The need to establish high qualifications for design practitioners is driven by the need for comprehensive knowledge about the proximate environment and emerging new design technologies.

Designers of skill, creative insight, and thorough technical expertise are required to protect the investments and safety of consumers – both in the contract and residential arenas.

To that end, ASID offers an educational career path to its members which is open to students, beginning practitioners and to experienced professionals. The Society's continuing education program is un-rivaled in terms of depth and scope – designers may avail themselves of some 40 professional development seminars conducted throughout the nation. These courses provide the technical and business skills necessary to keep abreast of the changes which are shaping the future of the profession and of the American interior.

More than ever before, as the field of interior design expands and becomes increasingly more complex, design professionals and their clients need an organization which can do two crucial things: first, properly and fairly represent them; secondly, provide a voice for legislation that will protect the public and enhance the practice of interior design. ASID – through its programs in communications, education, legislative and public affairs, membership and industry – provides that cohesive support and representation.

Today, the highest mark of the professional standard is conferred by the letters – ASID (American Society of Interior Designers). Through accredited education, documented experience, and adherence to a code of ethics, it is the ASID interior designer who commands the confidence of consumers and the respect of the professional design community. Professional members – the highest category of member-ship – are identified by the letters ASID after their names. Professional members must complete a national examination in addition to meeting criteria regarding education and experience required for Allied and Associate members.

Pale peach walls lend a soft atmosphere to this dining room, while the skirted chairs and glass-top dining table provide scale to balance the chandelier above. Interior design by ASID member Joseph Horan, photography by John Vaughan.

The Institute of Business Designers

The Institute of Business Designers is an internationally recognized organization representing interior design professionals who specialize in commercial and institutional design. IBD serves over 3,500 members in 30 chapters across the country. Professional members of the Institute have graduated from an approved college design program, practiced for a stipulated number of years, and passed the minimum competency examination administered by the National Council for Interior Design Qualification (NCIDQ).

The Institute of Business Designers was conceived in 1963 by members of the National Office Furnishings Association (NOFA) who met in Chicago to discuss the growing importance of the design professional to the office product industry. They subsequently formed an organization to provide a forum for designers who were affiliated with contract furnishing dealerships. The new organization grew in membership and in 1970 emerged as IBD, an independent organization representing professional contract interior designers.

In 1986, IBD adopted a mission statement which guides the organization's activities: "Leaders together, advance our profession."

The Institute is committed to advancing the profession of contract design by promoting higher standards, providing educational programming, and supporting legislation that protects the public through recognition of qualified design professionals.

The Institute supports its members' professional development through continuing educational programming which provides state-of-the-art information on contract design disciplines. IBD annually sponsors a national professional practice conference — "In the Business of Design" — and two of the nation's premier contract design competitions: the IBD/*Interior Design Magazine* Contract Design Competition and the IBD/*Contract Magazine* Product Design Competition.

In 1987 the Institute founded a national certification program for Contract Interior Designers. This self certification program for senior professionals in interior design is administered by the newly founded Governing Board for Contract Interior Design Standards. The Institute believes that professional certification is an important way to bring professionalism and excellence to the contract interior design industry.

The Institute also strongly supports licensing efforts that contain the five criteria endorsed by NCIDQ and ASID. We believe that both certification and licensing provide the public with important measurements of safe and productive interior environments.

IBD is governed by a Board of Directors comprised of one representative from each of the organization's 30 chapters and eight executive officers. Board members meet three times a year and service a two-year term. In addition, each of the chapters elects its own officers.

Adapted reuse transformed this warehouse into a two-level commercial space, with a suite of business offices situated above a lower level design and art studio. Interior design by IBD member Cynthia Leftwich, photography by Robert Suddarth.

The International Society of Interior Designers

The International Society of Interior Designers (ISID) was founded by a group of nine Los Angeles based professional interior designers and chartered in January 1979 in the State of California. A worldwide membership supports the following purposes:

- Legal recognition of professional interior designers in order to protect the health and welfare of the consumer and to protect against fraud and malpractice;

- Implementation of laws and studies in design to benefit aged, infirm and physically impaired;

- Ongoing education for the interior designer through seminars, lectures and academic courses;

- Development of educational programs for students in accredited schools of interior design, participation in apprenticeship and placement counseling;

- Scholarships and awards;

- Participation in an exchange of international design ideas, products and trends;

- Involvement in civic, community, national and international projects through technical advice and assistance to the deprived;

- Participation in restoration and preservation of historical, cultural and architectural sites;

- Development of liaisons, coordination of mutual goals and im-provement in lines of communication with schools of environmental design;

- And promotion of networking, on an international level, between designers, students, trade and related fields.

The ISID also sponsors:

- Lectures, seminars and conferences to stimulate and enrich members' careers.

- A networking system which provides members the opportunity to enjoy personal ties and long lasting relationships.

- International exchange to encourage communication amongst members in cities and countries throughout the world for professional assistance fellowship.

- Chapter activities, including civic, community and charitable projects, monthly meetings, social events and year round educational programs.

- Publication of newsletters, keeping members current as to news, calendars and other events.

- Design houses, which enable members to showcase their talents and products.

- Awards in Fellowship, Student Scholarship, Chapter, Personal Development, and Trade categories.

This contemporary design for the Optics by Victor boutique in Los Angeles
features a color scheme in grey and burgundy, dramatically bathed in spot lighting.
Interior design by ISID member Barbara Woolf, photography by Larry Carpp.

NORTH AMERICA: EAST

Anthony Antine, ISID, Formal Living Room, New Jersey

Charles J. Bommarito, ASID, Contemporary Living Room, Michigan

Janet Bourne, Columned Entry/Living Room, Virginia

Diane Boyer, ASID, Grand Bathroom, New Jersey

Carol Donayre Bugg, ASID, Country French Living Room, Maryland

Anne Cooper, Lady's Home Office, New Jersey

Martha O. Dalitzky, ASID, Contemporary Living/Dining Room, Massachusetts

Michael de Santis, ASID, Neoclassical Living Room, New York City

Susan Ley Dearborn, New England Kitchen, Massachusetts

Suellen DeFrancis, Carnegie Hill Living/Dining Room, New York

Iris DeMauro, Traditional Living Room, New York City

Robert Dirstein, Formal Drawing Room, Toronto

Trudy Dujardin, ASID, New England Study, Connecticut

Beverly Ellsley, 'Rustic Elegant' Kitchen, Connecticut

William R. Eubanks, Southern Drawing Room, Memphis

John Ford, FASID, Art Gallery/Living Room, Baltimore

Arlene Golub, ASID, Victorian Living Room, Baltimore

Mark Hampton, ASID, Edwardian Library, New York City

Charles Johnston, ASID, Traditional Southern Library, Atlanta

Adrienne Kamp, ISID, Contemporary Living Room, Chicago

Barbara LeVin, Manhattan *Pied-a-Terre*, New York City

Rod Maxwell, ISID, Contemporary Bedroom, Chicago

H. Glenn McGee, AIA, ASID, Resort Sitting Room/Bedroom, Florida

Carol Meltzer, ASID, Mirrored Dining Room, New York City

Anthony Michael, Contemporary Great Room, Chicago

Sandra Nunnerley, ASID, Manhattan Entry/Living Room, New York City

Gwen Pardun Rotolo, ISID, 'Versailles' Dining Room, Illinois

Darryl Savage, Neoclassical Entry/Living Room, Baltimore

Maureen Sullivan Stemberg, 'Paris Salon' Living Room, Boston

Lee Walsh, Traditional Living/Dining Room, Toronto

John Wendover, Traditional Dining Room, Montreal

From the Kips Bay Boys' and Girls' Club Decorator Showhouse: despite its grand dimensions, this living room remains intimate and inviting. Interior design: Michael de Santis, ASID. Photography: Jaime Ardiles-Arce.

Anthony Antine, ISID

*A*nthony Antine, a Charter Member of ISID, has served on the Board of Directors of the society's New York Chapter. He established his interiors firm in 1973 after his couturier clients demanded he design warm, comfortable environments for their homes, reflecting the clothes he created for them. He has done numerous private residences as well as restaurants, and hotels such as The Point Hotel on Saranack Lake. Mr. Antine has also designed a group of custom furniture pieces, one of which, a chaise based on the Victorian *téte-a-téte*, is featured here.

"*T*o begin the design of this living room, I used a double chaise to divide the awkwardly shaped room into three sections: a seating group near the fireplace, a desk area at the center of the room, and a media area with a mechanized bar and TV. Although I love period panelling, the room's 1920's era reproduction was not a good example, so I chose to paint it to set a soft field for the bold, over-scaled furnishings I wanted to use. Accents of gilt, and the Baccarat chandeliers give the room its sparkle. I feel my strong use of color and space are what make this room successful. I find that clients who select me prefer rooms that are relaxed but opulent; they understand how I feel about design and life."

Anthony Antine, ISID, Antine Associates
1028 Arcadian Way, Palisade, New Jersey 07024
Tel.: (201) 224-0315

Photography: Phillip H. Ennis (above), Peter Paige (right)

Charles J. Bommarito, ASID

A native of Detroit, Michigan, Charles Bommarito chose to establish his residential interior design firm in his home town. He is a graduate of Eastern Michigan University, where he received his Bachelor of Science in Interior Design. A Professional Member of the American Society of Interior Designers, Mr. Bommarito offers a full range of experience, knowledge and talent as he approaches each project with the commitment to create ideal environments for his clients.

"*I* t is hard to bridge from one style to another, and this was the situation I faced with this living room. The spacious ranch house was built in the 1950's, but featured a more contemporary style than usually found for the time and area. My client didn't care for modern styling, but I encouraged the owner to work with me since I had a design in mind that would be appealing, and would also correct a basic problem in the room.

"*D* espite its many windows, the room had a dark cast at any time of day, primarily due to the window treatments and traditional color palette used on the furnishings. The task presented to me was to open up the room, to give it a feeling of lightness and softness, while still maintaining a foothold in the traditional character that the client so desired. This was accomplished by a harmony of color, contrast and style. I used a complementary color scheme, selecting colors from the existing stonework of the fireplace. Lightness and balance were both enhanced by the contrast between the light-colored kidney-shaped sofas and the dark piano and writing desk. With the addition of carefully selected accessories, the client was extremely pleased with the interplay of contemporary-styled space and the warmth and character provided by the Oriental and traditional accents."

Charles J. Bommarito, ASID, National Interiors
19380 Ten Mile Road, Eastpointe, Michigan 48021
Tel: (313) 771-2260, Fax: (313) 771-2927

Janet Bourne

Commercial and residential designer Janet Bourne graduated with honors from Houston Community College where, in 1984, she received the interior design award. She began her career at Scandinavian Interiors and founded Janet Bourne Interiors in 1987. She has participated in two consecutive showcase homes, winning the award for Best Kitchen Design in 1990. Ms. Bourne has also participated in the Richmond Symphony Designer House, where she designed the master bath and created a hand-sculpted wall treatment. Her projects have been featured in *Home/Style*, *Richmond Surroundings Magazine*, the 1992 *Insiders Guide to Richmond* and numerous other publications.

"Serving as both a living area and music room, this room called for a feeling of classic elegance. I wanted each piece within the room to maintain its unique characteristics, while tying together the elegance of the whole. I began by mirroring the entire far wall, visually enlarging the room and amplifying the room's light and add dimension. I used a pair of columns at the room's entrance to create a sense of formal drama. Finished in a faux-marble, these columns separate the room from the two-story entry without blocking it as a source of light. For the room's colors, I chose the dynamic contrasts of a predominantly black and white palette. A minimal use of additional color completes this design, accented in the window treatments, floor coverings, fabrics and accessories."

Janet Bourne, Janet Bourne Interiors
3221 Lakewood Road, Glen Allen, Virginia 23060
Tel.: (800) 682-1251

Photography: Anne Gummerson

Diane Boyer, ASID

*A*fter receiving her B.F.A. from the University of Illinois, Diana Boyer went on to complete an M.S. at Pratt Institute and advanced studies at the New York School of Interior Design and Fashion Institute of Technology. A Professional Member of the American Society of Interior Designers, Ms. Boyer's interior design projects have been featured in books and numerous magazines, including *Interior Design* and *Interiors*. Her efforts in organizing ASID community and historical restoration projects were recognized in a White House ceremony in 1990.

"*I*ntricate woodwork and colors of the Victorian porches of Cape May, New Jersey, inspired this whimsical bath retreat. Originally a summer porch, the angled walls and low windows were enhanced with etched glass, hand-painted wall fabrics and custom-designed *faux* finish cabinetry. The white whirlpool for two is set in a fretwork canopy, surrounded by luxurious marble grooming areas. An inviting blend of exquisite antiques, contemporary art work and unexpected uses of color complete this private sanctuary of fanciful comfort."

Diane Boyer, ASID, Boyer-Cooper Interiors, Ltd.
32 Godwin Avenue, Midland Park, New Jersey 07432
Tel.: (201) 445-8412, Fax: (201) 445-2987

Photography: Phillip H. Ennis

Carol Donayre Bugg, ASID

*C*arol Bugg began her design education at the International Institute of Interior Design in Washington, DC, and continued on to the prestigious Parsons School of Design in Paris. Her career experience includes interior design positions at W & J Sloane, the H. Chambers Company, Stix Baer & Fuller, and developing Carol Donayre Bugg and Associates, a model home design company. Since 1984, she has been Vice President and Director of Design for Decorating Den Systems, Inc., a worldwide interior decorating franchise business with more than 1,200 units. Carol Bugg has lectured at the Smithsonian Institution and has appeared on both the NBC *"Today Show"* and the ABC *"Home"* show. Her first book, *Dream Rooms for Real People*, was published in 1990, and she is working on a new design book scheduled for publication in 1994.

*"T*he furnishings and colors for this room were inspired by my love for the south of France. I used a mixture of French antiques and contemporary pieces to create an elegant but informal European Country feeling. The finishing touches were flowered prints for the window treatments and the incorporation of family pictures, memorable treasures, books, and other special personal pieces. This room truly typifies my design style – every client is special, and every client has treasured items which I work into each room's design."

Carol Donayre Bugg, ASID, Decorating Den
7910 Woodmont Avenue, Bethesda, Maryland 20814-3058
Tel.: (800) 428-1366, (301) 652-6393, Fax: (301) 652-9017

Photography: Charles Maraia (above); Gordon Beall (opposite)

Anne Cooper

*A*ward-winning designer Anne Cooper started her professional career in California, then expanded her business to the East Coast. Known for sophisticated interiors with a European influence, Anne's creative combinations of color, fabrics, and exquisite antiques have been featured in numerous prestigious designer showcases and interior design publications.

"*C*olor sets the mood in this unique home office for an art dealer and working mother. Elegant yet functional, this room accommodates a computer work-center, a learning corner for her child, and a comfortable conversation area for client consultations. I wanted to create sophisticated window treatments to take advantage of the room's high ceiling and interesting window placement. The appealing blend of accessories and art work perfects a home office that is harmonious with all of the client's roles."

Anne Cooper, Boyer-Cooper Interiors, Ltd.
32 Godwin Avenue, Midland Park, New Jersey 07432
Tel.: (201) 445-8412, Fax: (201) 445-2987

Photography: Phillip H. Ennis

Martha O. Dalitzky, ASID

Martha Dalitzky graduated from the University of Massachusetts at Amherst and continued her studies at the University of Connecticut and Harvard Graduate School of Design. She has been active as a residential and commercial designer for over twenty-five years, and is the founder of the interior design firm Studio East. Her numerous projects can be seen throughout New England and Florida. Her work has been recognized and featured in many regional and national publications.

"**F**or this Massachusetts ranch-style home, I created an oasis in rose, sand, and sea green. To create a sense of tranquility, I first carpeted the entire space in a fisherman's knit pattern. The natural wool of the carpet echos the sand and shell tones of the marble fireplace. The living area features back-to-back sofas in a water lily printed cotton. The water birds on the Oriental screen in the background accent the seaside villa theme. In the spectacular dining room, I used a Venetian glass chandelier of cascading prisms to reflect onto the mirrored table. Throughout this room, the presence of natural materials creates the timeless, peaceful quality I was striving for."

Martha O. Dalitzky, ASID, Studio East Inc.
15 Benton Drive, P.O. Box 487, East Longmeadow, Massachusetts 01028
Tel.: (413) 525-4850, Fax: (413) 567-8971

Photography: James A. Langone

Michael de Santis, ASID

Michael de Santis has participated in numerous design showcase homes, including the prestigious Kips Bay Boys' and Girls' Club Showhouse and the Rogers Memorial Library Designer Showhouse in Southampton, New York. He has lectured at the Smithsonian Institution and has been published in *Architectural Digest* and other major interior design publications many times during his career.

"*T*his project gave me the opportunity to work with a room that is architecturally dominated by an extremely high ceiling. This high ceiling essentially designated the scale of the entire room. I didn't want it to look too traditional, but I did want to introduce some unusual elements such as the four-foot high 18th century French carved wood figures depicting the four seasons. By placing them on high pedestals I emphasized the height of the room. Instead of using paintings on the walls, I chose to have wall murals done in the style of Georgio de Chirico. The room seemed to call for a somewhat grand look, thus I used lots of antique accessories paired with contemporary furniture, the placement of which allows for fluid movement, yet has a large seating capacity."

Michael de Santis, Michael de Santis, Inc.
1110 Second Avenue at 58th Street, New York, New York 10022
Tel.: (212) 753-8871, Fax: (212) 935-7777

Photography: Phillip H. Ennis

Susan Ley Dearborn

Susan Ley Dearborn graduated from Vassar College, and later received a degree in Interior Design from Mt. Ida College. Her client base is in the New England area, with a primary focus on residential and executive office space. Ms. Dearborn's volunteer projects include Boston's Junior League Show House, the York Maine Show House and the Fenway Community Health Center.

"My challenge in this kitchen family area was to create a warm, relaxing elegance by softening the architecture's formal elements. To enhance and soften the custom wood, I hung walls and windows with a classic French Brunschwig & Fils fabric, rich in greens, persimmons and golden yellows. The same intensity and color hues are found in the Portuguese needlepoint rug and in the fabrics used on the Solutions custom designed chairs and chaise."

Susan Ley Dearborn, Allied ASID, Solutions by Susan Ley Dearborn
30 Cliff Road, Wellesley, Massachusetts 02181
Tel.: (617) 235-2920

Photography: Anna D. Shaw

Suellen DeFrancis

Numbering the New York Yacht Club, Nippon Steel USA, Mitsubishi Housing and Asahi Breweries among her clients, Suellen DeFrancis provides architectural and architectural interior services to corporations and individuals. She holds a Masters degree in Urban Design from the City College Graduate Center, as well as Bachelors and Bachelor of Science degrees in Architecture from City College School of Architecture and Environmental Studies.

"Cultural diversity is just one concept I used in designing a simple but classical atmosphere for this Carnegie Hill condominium in New York City. I had already had the privilege of designing my clients' Tokyo home, so an added design factor was to choose furniture, fabrics, and colors that would be suitable when moved to Tokyo. But foremost was a desire for comfort and intimacy. Since my clients shared my aversion to the 'coordinated' look, I used contrasting colors to complement the classical lines of the furniture. I wanted to assure that there was no break in textures or materials from space to space, and used only natural fabrics – wool, silk, and cotton. I decided upon dining chairs covered in blue-on-blue hand-screened silk, salon chairs in burgundy and cream hand-screened silk, and the sofa in a muted cotton floral print. As final accessories, I selected occasional lamps to produce soft lighting for the conversation area, accented by Japanese-style cushions at both ends of a glass-top coffee table. The completed design is one suitable for either Oriental or Western entertaining."

Suellen DeFrancis, Suellen DeFrancis Architectural Interiors, Inc.
Post Office Box 247, Scarsdale, New York 10583
Tel.: (914) 472-8013, Fax: (914) 472-5235

Photography: Norman McGrath

Iris DeMauro

O f Japanese and Italian-American heritage, Iris DeMauro was born and raised in Japan. She was educated in Tokyo at Sophia University, and then the University of California Berkeley where she received a degree in psychology. She moved to New York to receive another degree in Environmental Design from Parson's School of Design. She founded her interior design firm, Iris DeMauro, Inc. in 1980. She is president and co-founder of Archetype Gallery in New York's historical Soho District. In 1987, she opened

GEO International, which specializes in furnishings created from fossilized stones and marbles. Her major projects include renovation of the Sheraton Hotel in Okinawa, and her work has been published worldwide.

"A s this interior reflects, my design philosophy lies in elegant combinations of the traditional, the archeological, and the avante garde. The juxtaposition of extraordinary, antique materials and traditional period pieces harmonizes to produce a mysterious, exotic, and thought-provoking quality. In this room I combined Louis XVI antiques with unusual antiquities such as the 'Warring States' bronze vessel, 475-221 B.C., on the black fossil stone pedestal, while using contemporary artist Carol Bruns' bronze 'Light Bearer' candelabra and figures to serve as the focal point of the window. To deepen the room's mystery, I added the perforated table lamp by Warren Muller and the painting by avante garde artist Michael Abrams."

Iris DeMauro, Iris DeMauro, Inc.
115 Mercer Street, New York, New York 10012
Tel.: (212) 226-7766, Fax: (212) 529-5654

Photography: Felipe Morales

Robert Dirstein

A native of Chesley, Ontario, Robert Dirstein completed his education at the Ontario College of Art in 1951. His career as a residential interior designer has now spanned 40 years. For most of that time, since 1956, he has been president of his own independent interior design firm, Dirstein Robertson Limited in Toronto. His major projects include three palaces in Saudi Arabia, as well as commissions in Florida, California, and New York. Robert Dirstein's work has been published in *Interior Design*, the British edition of *House & Garden*, and *Architectural Digest*.

"*T*his room allowed me to indulge my specialty in the use of French and English furniture. My first aim in designing this traditional drawing room was to carry its dramatic architectural features — tall ceilings and three large, bowed windows overlooking a private walled garden — to full advantage. To this end, I installed a spectacular Irish Chippendale breakfront overflowing with botanical porcelain. The breakfront and the French aubusson carpet dominate the room, with French and English artwork enhancing the combination. The rather imposing mirror calls attention to the height of the walls, as does the large painting above the mantle. Intimacy is restored by the low hanging chandelier, the furniture placement and the rich, warm gold tones of the wall treatment, picture frames, moldings and draperies. I completed this room with an unusual pair of 18th century Venetian bodice-back chairs, which add to the distinctiveness of all the room's elements."

Robert Dirstein, Dirstein Robertson Limited
77 Yorkville Avenue, Toronto, Ontario, Canada M5R 1C1
Tel.: (416) 961-6211, Fax: (416) 961-5537

Photography: Peter Vitale

Trudy Dujardin, ASID

*T*rudy Dujardin received her B.S. in Art Education and Fine Arts from Southern Connecticut State College, and did her graduate studies at New York University and Parsons School of Design. She has won numerous awards for her interior design projects, and was featured on "Bob Vila's Home Again" (CBS) twice in 1991.

"*I* combined old world panache with high technology in this New England study. This room gave me the opportunity to create subtle contrasts in color, style and period. Light pine, Swedish antiques and white marbleized moldings add contrast to the rich, brown walls. I used brown tinted mirror and glass in the bar area to add sparkle to the warmth of the room; the nautical accent pieces complete the overall feeling of a classic Connecticut study."

Trudy Dujardin, Trudy Dujardin Interiors
3 Sylvan Road South, Westport, Connecticut 06880
(203) 222-1019

Photography: Bill Rothschild

Beverly Ellsley

*B*everly Ellsley is well-known for both interior design and the design of custom cabinetry. She is president of Beverly Ellsley, Inc. based in Westport, Connecticut. In 1985, Ms. Ellsley was the recipient of the Designer Showhouse Award from *House Beautiful*. She participated in the Hospice Decorator Showhouse in 1988 and the Kips Bay Decorator Showhouses of 1985 and 1992. Ms. Ellsley's work has appeared in many publications including *House Beautiful*, *Good Housekeeping*, *Ladies Home Journal* and the *New York Times*, and was also featured on the cover of the March 1993 issue of *Country Living*.

"*T*his project, from the Chieftains Showhouse, posed the exciting challenge of creating a kitchen from what had been a working dairy barn. I began by removing the hayloft to expose the dramatic open ceiling. Both ceiling and walls were then painted white to brighten the area, and a huge window was placed where the hayloft doors had been. To level the floor, I had to have the cow troughs filled in; the cement was then hand-painted to look like large tiles. Because my firm manufactures custom millwork and cabinetry, I had immediate access to the items required during the next phase of this project. I designed a large pine island to provide storage, counter space and a place for the rangetop, with one end overhanging to form a snack bar. Because the area is so large, I combined two types of cabinetry to avoid redundancy. These were given an antiqued green finish in contrast to the natural wood tones of the countertops and moldings. As accessories, a few milk cans on the ledge at loft-level are reminders of the room's humble origins, while the iron chandelier epitomizes the rustic elegance I strove to maintain."

Beverly Ellsley, Beverly Ellsley, Inc.
175 Post Road, Westport, Connecticut 06880
Tel: (203) 227-1157, Fax: (203) 227-6681

Photography: Bill Rothschild

William R. Eubanks

*A*fter a successful partnership of fifteen years, William Eubanks established William R. Eubanks Interior Design in 1990. The firm specializes in 17th, 18th and early 19th century English and Continental antiques as well as interior design.

"*T*his warm and vibrant drawing room was designed for a color-loving client with an insatiable appetite for collecting exotica. Fringed draperies of Scalamandré silk frame one of a pair of 19th-century Venetian blackamoors, while Empire candelabras sit beside a *chinoiserie* box. High ceilings and tall doorways allowed the use of well-proportioned mouldings. The Queen Anne *chinoiserie* double-bonnet secretary displays several collections including Sevres figures of Napoleon's marshals. My client describes entering this room as like 'stepping into my own jewelbox'."

William R. Eubanks, William R. Eubanks Interior Design
1516 Union Avenue, Memphis, Tennessee 38104
Tel.: (901) 272-1825, Fax: (901) 272-1845

Photography: Tina Freeman

John Ford, FASID

*A*fter receiving his degrees from Johns Hopkins University and the Maryland Institute, College of Art, John Ford founded his own design firm in 1962. As an art specialist, Mr. Ford is a member of the Smithsonian Institution Freer Gallery of Art's Board of Advisors and serves on the Asia Society's executive committee. Because he is a private collector of art as well as a consultant to individual collectors and museums, John Ford's work is highlighted by the planning and execution of interior designs that incorporate the arts of all cultures. His projects have been published in *Interiors Magazine*, *Interior Design*, *Better Homes and Gardens*, *House and Garden*, and numerous other publications.

"*T*he focus in conceiving this forty by eighteen-foot gallery/living room was the incorporation of my clients' impressive collection of Indian and Himalayan art objects into a unified, contemporary presentation compatible with their busy lifestyles. I first wanted to arrange the collection as an integral part of the overall design. I began by designing a built-in wall unit and free-standing pedestals specifically for the bronze and stone sculptures. Lighting for the built-in unit is controlled behind an independent vertical baffle. To complement the artwork and traditional architecture, I employed the muted colors and textures of tie-dyed velvet, natural leather and grasscloth. The contemporary furniture is arranged in casual groupings which provide comfort for evenings at home and entertaining while allowing close inspection, even from a seated position, of many of the small paintings hung along the knee wall. Although the art is everywhere, the drama it creates does not overwhelm the space."

John Ford, FASID, John Ford Associates, Inc.
2601 North Charles Street, Baltimore, Maryland 21218
Tel.: (410) 467-9400, Fax: (410) 243-3451

Photography: Buzzy Muvsho

Arlene Golub, ASID

*A*rlene Golub continued her studies at The International Institute of Interior Design in Washington, D.C., after receiving her Art History degree from George Washington University. She has done major projects for Delta Air Lines, Standard Oil of Indiana, Margolis Sakayan Law Offices, The National Symphony and antique dealer showhouses. As well as conducting lecture series, her work has been published in *Interior Design, House and Garden, The Washington Post,* and *Designers Portfolio.*

"*I* decorated this handsomely paneled library in 18th century Louis XVI French furnishings. I chose rich wood furnishings and accessories that showed much gold and ormolu, including the lovely grained wood bookcase with gold trim. The warm red and gold fabrics covering the fine period pieces add elegance, glamour, and charm. The fine history of the room is set off by the modern plexiglas pieces and the leopard skin patterns of the rug and ottoman."

Arlene Golub, Arlene Golub Interiors
6409 Tilden Lane, Rockville, Maryland 20852
Tel.: (301) 881-6008, Fax: (301) 881-6008

Photography: Gordon Beall

Mark Hampton

*A*fter training with such design luminaries as David Hicks and Mrs. Henry Parrish, Mark Hampton founded his own design firm in New York City in 1976. His major projects include Washington's Blair House, the National Observatory, the Oval Office of the White House, Gracie Mansion in New York, and showcase houses throughout the United States. Mr. Hampton's work has been published in newspapers and magazines across America. A noted expert on interior design, he is the author of *Mark Hampton on Decorating*.

"*I* wanted to create the mood of an Edwardian library dressed for summer. The walls of this large, nearly cubical room are black-brown, with blue added to the paint to avoid a mushy chocolate tone. Since I dislike dead-white in a room, I used a vanilla shade for the ornamental woodwork defining the room's borders. The large, old-fashioned English furnishings were covered in a creamy self-striped cotton from Brunschwig & Fils. Ivory straw matting was placed on the floor and cream-colored gauze was used in the window treatments.

"*T*hroughout the room, I employed dark Georgian mahogany pieces to balance the lightness of the tufted upholstery and bamboo. The dynamic contrasts of light and dark in this space are reflected in the eighteenth-century landscape above the sofa, painted in Italy by Pieter van Lindt. Further counterpoint is provided by the Coromandel screen from Frederick Victoria which flanks the painting and extends its colorings. The play of shades suggests colorfulness in a room which, nonetheless, makes use of a rather restrained palette. The result is a finely tuned English sitting room, chicly Edwardian, yet appropriate to modern tastes."

Mark Hampton, Mark Hampton, Inc.
654 Madison Avenue, New York, New York 10021
Tel.: (212) 753-4110, Fax: (212) 758-2079

Photography: Peter Vitale

Chip Johnston, ASID

*R*esidential projects are the focus of Chip Johnston's Atlanta-based interior design firm. Educated at Emory University and the University of North Carolina at Chapel Hill, Mr. Johnston gained valuable interior design experience in a variety of positions before opening his own firm in 1979. As a Professional Member of the American Society of Interior Designers, he has received a number of accolades from his peers, including an Industry Foundation Citation, a Medalist Award, and three Presidential Citations. His memberships in the National Trust for Historic Preservation, the Cooper-Hewitt Museum and several fine arts organizations speak highly of his commitment to a professional, cultured approach to every project.

"*Q*uiet comfort was the goal for this handsome mahogany-cabineted library. We wanted an atmosphere suited to conversation or deep concentration while working with the concealed computer equipage. The ceiling-high shelves on three walls are detailed with graceful arches and fluted pilasters. The light from a chandelier given by a friend of the client is supplanted with lamps and the natural illumination from the large bay window. Deep peach draperies and wall frame the paisley covered loveseat, and lighter accents include the antique Chinese porcelains, the matting of the Tobias lithograph, and even the colorful book spines. The antique Mahal rug pulls all the colors together for a warmly inviting room."

Charles "Chip" A. Johnston, Jr., Chip Johnston Interiors
2996 Grandview Avenue, N.E., Suite 300, Atlanta, Georgia 30305
Tel.: (404) 231-4141

Photography: David Schilling

Adrienne Kamp, ISID

*A*drienne Kamp, ISID, is a graduate of Roosevelt University and the International Academy of Merchandising and Design. Her award-winning projects have been nationally published, and she presently serves on the Board of Directors of the International Society of Interior Designers, Illinois Chapter. Adrienne Kamp lectures for many civic and social organizations on design/space planning, and she is listed in the 1992-1993 International Edition of *Who's Who in Interior Design.*

"*I* took the breathtaking views of Chicago's lake front and brought them indoors with an eight-panel screen made of rich bronze, brass and mother-of-pearl inlaid on an ebony background. Snow-white leather sectional sofas, interestingly angled, began the overall flow of space planning. Superb artwork is found throughout the room and its furnishings, from a custom designed rough stainless steel dining table base to soaring sculpture pieces. The triangular shaped banquette provides intimate seating for eight to twelve guests. I created the dramatic and elegant window treatment using soft unstructured swags, knotted ends, and two tiered panels which puddle on the floor. Tucked-away lighting haloes strategic areas. Replacing a wall with sliding bleached oak panels continues the open feeling into the small adjoining den/guest bedroom. The striking color scheme of black, white, and deep teals enriches this classic, contemporary residence."

Adrienne Kamp, ISID, K&R Interiors, Ltd.
6858 North Latrobe Street, Skokie, Illinois 60077
Tel.: (708) 674-6858, Fax: (708) 673-2634

Photography: David Rigg

Barbara LeVin

A graduate of the Willsey Institute of Interior Design, Barbara LeVin has designed numerous residential and office interiors throughout New York, Vermont and New Mexico. Her projects have appeared in such publications as *Traditional Home, Better Homes & Gardens, Home Magazine* and *Newsday Magazine.*

"*I*n this Manhattan *pied-a-terre*, my intention was to create a tranquil, elegant yet comfortable retreat with a warm European tone. The room's key architectural feature – the wall of French doors and windows – provides abundant natural light from the adjoining garden. I selected rich floral fabrics, plants and flowers along with the impressionist oil painting above the sofa to accentuate the sunny garden view. To enhance the design's eclectic appeal, I chose a mix of French and English furniture and accessories. A late 19th-century French butler's tray serves as a coffee table, adorned with 19th-century boule balls, also from France. The circa 1870 Louis XV-style dining table and chairs are light cherry/fruitwood and display decorative French terrines and a wool paisley fringed cloth. Also French are the quimper fruit compote and goose atop the *pannetiere* (bread cabinet) above the dining table. The brass twisted candlestick lamps are English, as are the garden dog figures and 19th-century needlepoint fireplace stool. The wrought iron wall ornament is from Spain. A sisal rug anchors the main conversation area. The result is a refined city setting with a fresh country character."

Barbara LeVin, Barbara LeVin Interiors
120 East 56th Street, Suite 515, New York, New York, 10022
Tel.: (212) 688-9070, Fax: (212) 688-9069

Photography: David Phelps

Rod Maxwell, ISID

*R*od Maxwell graduated from Rockford College, receiving his Bachelor's Degree in Fine Arts. After five years as a Display Designer, he founded his own design firm in 1980.

"*T*o create this romantic bedroom, I began with the walls, which were sponged in four subtle tones of ecru and then stenciled in a fretwork frieze highlighted with interwoven vines and blossoms. The room's focal point is the canopied bed, where I used brushed steel ivy rods and finials. Stamped cotton damask for the bed's headboard and dust ruffle, along with luxurious fabrics for the chair and bed pillows come together to create the sumptuous feeling I knew this room should have."

Rod Maxwell, R.A. Maxwell, Inc.
5461 N. East River Road, Suite 901, Chicago, Illinois 60656
Tel.: (312) 693-2857, Fax: (312) 693-6620

Photography: Jon Miller of Hedrich Blessing (room); David Rigg (portrait and vignette)

H. Glenn McGee, AIA, ASID

A native of South Carolina, Glenn McGee graduated from Clemson University with a Bachelor of Architecture degree. His thirty-year career has spanned seven states and includes travel and study in Italy, Switzerland, Austria, Canada, the Bahamas and Saudi Arabia. A member of both the AIA and the ASID, Mr. McGee's office is now in Florida, where he specializes in custom residential design work. In addition to his prestigious career as a designer, Mr. McGee has been active as a lecturer on Interior Design and Architectural History at the University of South Carolina.

"*T*his ever-so-small hideaway on John's Island in Indian River Shores, Florida challenged me to take a very small space and create a comfortable, intimate bedroom and sitting room. Since the room had to accomplish several functions, I kept the architectural work light and simple. Three paneled mirrors at the head of the bed reflect light from the bay windows, creating an airy, spacious feeling. The color above the chair railing is a pale lemon yellow, accomplished by an overlay of glaze on white. With the ambience of the room completed, I brought in a Persian carpet, loveseat and a favorite reading chair, and arranged them directly in front of the windows to form the 'sitting room' without obstructing the line of vision from the bed area. Then all that was left was to add a few other favorite pieces and the accessory items that complete a good design."

H. Glenn McGee, AIA, ASID, McGee-Howle & Associates, Architects, Inc.
2801 Ocean Drive, Suite 302, Vero Beach, Florida 32963
Tel.: (407) 231-4222, Fax: (407) 231-4311

Photography: Kevin M. Gorman

Carol Meltzer, ASID

Carol Meltzer studied liberal arts at the F.I.T. School of Interior Design. She began her career as an interior designer with Nishho-Iwai and is currently president of P.T.M. Interiors in New York City. She has been a participating designer for the Long Island Guggenheim estate, as well as the 1989 New York City Showcase. Her projects have been published in the *New York Post*, the *New York Times*, and *The Designer*.

"As this dining room reveals, my style focuses on the environmental sense produced by blending natural products such as wood, stone, glass and metal with traditional art and antiquities. I wanted to achieve an aesthetic balance, giving my client an open and inviting atmosphere for both casual and formal dining. I began by installing mirrored panels to visually double the room's depth. I custom designed a deco-inspired chandelier of mirror and chrome to enhance the ceiling and complement the striking Lalique table. To finish this room in final detail, I have created 'Tablescapes', customized table decorations of etched glass and lacquered wood, to add an individual elegance to each place setting."

Carol Meltzer, ASID, P.T.M. Interiors
51 East 82nd Street, New York, New York 10028
Tel.: (212) 737-5139, Fax: (212) 737-5139

California Office:
64345 Via Risso, Palm Springs, California 92262
Tel.: (619) 322-0702, Fax: (619) 322-6084

Photography: James Levin

65

Anthony Michael

Specializing in residential, commercial and architectural design, Anthony Michael is president of his Chicago-based design firm. Mr. Michael has had many of his interiors published in newspapers and magazines, including the *Chicago Tribune, Chicago Sun Times, Builder Architect, Kitchen & Bath Concepts, Bon Appetit* and *Audio/Video Interiors*. He was recognized by the *Chicago Sun Times* as Designer of the Year in 1986, and by *Monitor* magazine as Retail Designer of the Year in 1992.

"Throughout the design of this great room, I focused upon creating a comfortable and inviting entertainment area my clients would enjoy and appreciate for many years. Striking in its spaciousness, this room's dimensions are emphasized by the high ceiling, columnar facade, and arched entrance. To accentuate the urban sophistication of this architecture, I used soft pale colors throughout the room. The sofa fabric, carpeting, wall finishes, and even the ceiling fans are in subtle and similar hues. For furnishings, sectional sofa units were arranged to accommodate both large and small groups, with additional seating provided by large ottomans. The black marble coffee table tops offer a dark contrast to the room's otherwise pale tones, and accessories include numerous candles, sculptures, and large decorative vases. A dramatic use of lighting completed this design, with eclipse fixtures on the walls, recessed spot lighting in the soffits and ceiling, and vertically-directed basin fixtures positioned just above eye level."

Anthony Michael, Interior Design, Ltd.
844 West Erie, Chicago, Illinois 60622
Tel.: (312) 243-2430, Fax: (312) 243-3651

Photography: Cort Wilson

Sandra Nunnerley, ASID

*S*andra Nunnerley was born and raised in New Zealand. After obtaining her Bachelor of Fine Arts in Architecture Degree from the University of Sydney, Australia, she moved to New York City and worked with Marlborough and Nancy Hoffman Galleries before establishing her own design firm in 1981. Sandra Nunnerley's work deftly combines exquisite antiques with period-influenced contemporary pieces – many of which she designs herself, incorporating original proportions and detailing with unexpected colorations, textures and materials. All carefully reflect the lifestyle and taste of her clients.

*T*he Kips Bay Boys' and Girls' Club Showhouse has featured rooms designed by Sandra Nunnerley in 1984, 1988, and 1992. Her work has been published in *Architectural Digest, Vogue Decoration, Maison et Jardin, Interior Design, Metropolitan Home*, and *HG*.

"*T*his Manhattan duplex was designed for a married couple, he being Swedish, she being American. With the apartment restored to its original condition, we created a neoclassical feeling while blending the best of both cultures. What resulted was a very relaxing, tranquil atmosphere with traditional detailing. American antiques with European influences such as Beidermeier offered the best of both worlds."

Sandra Nunnerley, Sandra Nunnerley Inc.
112 East 71st Street, New York, New York 10021
Tel: (212) 472-9341, Fax (212) 472-9346

Photography: Jaime Ardiles-Arce

Gwen Rotolo, ISID

*A*n Interior Design graduate of both Harper College and the Art Institute of Chicago, Gwen Rotolo began her design career in 1974. She spent several years as a custom designer for Boston's Cabot House, and five years as head interior designer for a Chicago-area firm. In 1985 she founded her own firm, Interiors by Gwen, in Palatine, Illinois and Scottsdale, Arizona. She has become a member of "Who's Who International" since opening her second Scottsdale location. Ms. Rotolo is an Allied Member of the American Society of Interior Designers and a Professional Member of the International Society of Interior Designers. Her work has been published in both the magazine and home sections of the *Chicago Tribune*, and her interior design work for Walter Payton was featured in *Ebony* magazine. Ms. Rotolo has participated in numerous Design Showcase Houses throughout the Chicago area.

"*I*n the dining room of this South Barrington home I strove for reminiscence of the 'Hall of Mirrors' at Versailles. The architectural focal point of the room is the recessed octagonal ceiling. This unusual shape, accented with indirect lighting, seemed to call for a dramatic beveled mirror. Combined with the Strauss crystal chandelier, the mirror creates a sparkling atmosphere as the lights refract and play off one another. I selected a lucite dining table to allow the clear top and bevel-columned base to add to the play of glass, mirror and light. Gracing the table are a Lalique bust vase filled with pink and rose silk peonies, and two Lalique swans swimming on mirrors toward the host and hostess. I had the chairs finished in gold leaf and upholstered in a Schumacher rose damask fabric. The French legs on the side chairs were gilded to match, and upholstered in a gold-on-white quilted linen. The splendid screen from Rozmallin adds depth and architectural interest to the corner of the room, and is balanced by a silk ficus tree in a gold leaf fishbowl atop a rosewood Oriental stand. The column motif established in the screen and table unites with the 'Hall of Mirrors' theme with the mirror on the rear wall. Beneath this mirror I placed an antique rams-leg console table with green marbled top. As a final accent, I selected an Erté statue to place between the gold candlesticks, and situated it in such a way that it appears to be descending the 'stairway' of the mirror's frame."

Gwen Pardun Rotolo, ISID, Interiors by Gwen

43 W. Robertson, Palatine, Illinois 60067
Tel.: (800) 354-GWEN (354-4936)

10115 E. Mt. View Road, Suite 1101, Scottsdale, Arizona 85858
Tel.: (602) 661-1952, Fax: (602) 661-1952

Photography: Steve Hall, Hedrich-Blessing

Darryl Savage

Darryl Savage was born in Washington, DC and educated at the New School for Social Research in New York. During his fourteen years as a designer, he has completed residential and commercial projects throughout the Mid-Atlantic region, and has won numerous awards for his work.

"My goal was to create a room which combined great comfort and simplicity with a sense of style and grandeur. Built as a spec house, this home's living room/foyer lacked the graceful proportions so important to good design. I began by removing walls, heightening doorways, and adding columns and custom millwork. The living room now opens freely into the foyer, creating an unimpeded flow of space and movement. The foyer area features a grand piano and a large Napolean III mirror flanked by a pair of antique tole urns on pedestals. The neoclassical mirror adds visual depth to the room and reflects the garden statue and columns leading into the living room area. Here I used a round tooled leather table to anchor the room, accompanied by a pair of camelback loveseats. To complete the room I used 18th century engravings, fine art and antiques mingled with natural materials of sisal, wood floors and linen silk."

Darryl Savage, DHS Designs
5530 Wisconsin Avenue, Suite 1610, Chevy Chase, Maryland 20815
Tel.: (301) 858-6391, Fax: (301) 913-2037

Photography: Anne Gummerson

Maureen Sullivan Stemberg

Specializing in residential and hotel interior design, Maureen Sullivan Stemberg has offices in both Boston and Palm Beach, Florida. Among her major projects are the Trump Plaza Penthouse, the award-winning Mahaney Baseball Clubhouse at the University of Maine, and Club Collette in Palm Beach. Her work has been published in *Interior Visions* and other design publications, and in 1992 she received the 'Top 20 Worldwide' Award for hotel design.

"When designing the large living room of this Boston condominium, I strove for the feeling of a Paris salon. To achieve this 'evening in Paris' atmosphere, I splashed the room in champagne colors, added accessories like the gilded, whitewashed Empire mirror and ornate fruited sconces with slags and bows, and designed the pillows with plenty of tassels and trim. Overhead, a soffit was built in with recessed lighting diffused by a curved ceiling. The salon-like ambience was completed with the collection of tea sets, tea caddies, and Venetian-glass boxes."

Maureen Sullivan Stemberg, Maureen Sullivan Stemberg Interior Design
211 Berkley Street, Boston, Massachusetts 02116   *Palm Beach Office:*
Tel.: (617) 536-8464, Fax: (617) 536-1750   *(407) 659-7126*

Photography: Peter Vitale (room), B.C. Kagan (portrait)

Lee Walsh

An accomplished designer, Lee Walsh utilizes her expertise as a professional artist to stimulate her keen sense of color and composition. She taught color theory and art at Loyalist College, and later incorporated this knowledge into the decorating classes she taught while working as a designer for various firms in Ottawa. Ms. Walsh opened her own firm in 1987, and personally designs many custom items used in her interiors.

"Original watercolors established both the color palette and garden theme I chose for this room, where one has the option of a formal dining area or overall living room capacity. I selected a lively floral pattern of coral red, pink, yellow and green on a white background for the skirted parsons chairs at the dining table, then pulled these colors into the living area with the two-toned mahogany *bergére* and the customized tufted ottoman by Silva's upholstery of Toronto. Black-piped, coral *moire* covering the pillows on the white damask love seat echo the color of the hand-painted antique secretary. Fresh white woodwork and off-white carpet is used throughout the area, which, with the neutral creams of the window treatments, directs the eye to the focal point of the seating arrangement and floral fabrics. A wrought iron room divider positioned between two white pillars was selected to create a trellis effect, adorned with preserved roses from Roseworks Preserved Flowers of Kingston. To complete the garden-like theme, I chose a floral and fruit tapestry tablecloth complemented with floral and white porcelain dishes."

Lee Walsh, Lee Walsh Interiors/Interiors by Design
P.O. Box 64590, Unionville, Ontario L3R OM9, Canada
Tel.: (416) 470-6122, Fax (416) 470-7448

Photography: Lorne Chapman

John Wendover

*J*ohn Wendover was born in Grimsby, United Kingdom, and emigrated to Canada in 1952. He graduated in Art History (Licence es Arts) with honors from McGill University. Mr. Wendover's principal works include upscale residences and executive suites with extensive art collections, government collection displays and museums, and the authentication of works from antiquity.

"*M*y client wanted his extensive collection housed in a formal but comfortable townhouse dining area. Most of the accent pieces took over a year to find and acquire. Major elements include wall coverings and draperies from Couperin, Chinese Tang shorn silk carpet, Louis XVI set by Pentier, paintings by Vermeer and contemporary artist Jean-Pierre Lafrance, chandelier by Schoenbeck, bronze 'La Liseuse' by Carrier-Belleuze, Rodin's teacher, mantel clock in marble and ormolu by Perrier from Malmaison. Other pieces include a solid gold monstrance (Quebec 1756) and a new age crystal sculpture 'Rock Cavern' by Rose Francis. The place settings are from the Ambassador Series by Lennox, the silver by Paul Revere and the crystal are of the Gallia pattern. Partially hidden in the corner is a Pompeian bronze of Antiochus VI Grypos, Satrap of Pompei with a Louis XVI gilt wood and marble console displaying a marble bust of Antinous from the IVth century AD. Finally the whole room is reflected in a sculpted gilt wood mirror from the XVIth century once housed in the library of the Hermitage."

John Wendover, Les Concepts Décoratifs Wendover Inc.
3875 Saint-Urbain, Suite 611, Montréal, Québec, Canada H2W 1V1
Tel: (514) 281-2073, Fax: (514) 844-8843, (514) 769-5618

Photography: Jose Bouthillette

NORTH AMERICA: WEST

Jack Adams, Marbled Living/Dining Room, Honolulu

Michael Anthony, Cosmopolitan Living Room, San Francisco

Douglas Bartoli, Early California Bedroom, Santa Barbara

Cordelia Cortes, Living/Dining Room, Mexico City

Roger Dobbel, ASID, Contemporary Study, San Francisco

Allison Holland, ASID, Island Living Room, Honolulu

Joseph P. Horan, ASID, Showcase Bedroom, San Francisco

Norma King, Ranch House Living Room, Texas

Patricia Klee, Grand Music Hall/Sunroom, Santa Barbara

Pat Larin, ASID, Showcase Living Room, San Francisco

Cheryl Monroe, ASID, Classical Foyer/Living Room, Seattle

Walter Nelson, ASID, Country Bedroom, San Diego

Penni Paul, Contemporary Entertainment Room, Beverly Hills

Jenny Real, Post-Modern Dining/Living Room, Mexico City

Gloria Roberts, ISID, Traditional Dining Room, Riverside

Judy Robins, Contemporary Living Room, Denver

Mary Sorenson, Library/Music Room, Texas

Edward Turrentine, ASID, Grand Pavilion/Salon, Pasadena

Carol Wharton, ISID, Hilltop Living Room, Rolling Hills Estates

Barbara Woolf, ISID, Red Russian Living Room, Beverly Hills

Overstuffed sofas and matching ottoman are accented by the white tile floor and a profusion of plants in this Palm Springs condominium. Interior design: Carol Meltzer, ASID. Photography: James Levin.

Jack Adams, ASID

*B*orn in Abilene, Texas, Jack Adams received his bachelor's degree from West Point, a B.A. from the Art Center College of Design, and did post-graduate work at a number of other schools and universities. He was a project designer for Richard Crowell Associates for three years, and then worked as director of interior design for Media 5 Architects, and was also interior design-er and marketing director for Dale Keller Associates. Since 1977, Mr. Adams has been Principal Designer and President of Adams Design, Inc., in Honolulu. His projects include the Mauna Kea Villas, the Sheraton Princeton in Kauai, the Bank of Honolulu, and the Hawaiian Monarch Hotel. Mr. Adams is a Professional Member of the American Society of Interior Designers, and his work has been featured in numerous design-related publications, most recently in *Island Home Magazine*.

"*T*his expansive room gave me a rare opportunity to design a private residence with the latitude usually only avail-able in resort hotel projects. Luxurious and spacious, this interior was designed with the formal entertaining of dignitaries in mind. I wanted to create an atmosphere in which an English lord could dine with Russian royalty. Begining with the floors, I selected a beautiful Italian marble. The creme and accenting burgundy stone was laid in a sweeping pattern in the living area, contrasted with a straight, more formal design in the dining space. Antique rugs were then inset in most spaces except the dining area, where I used a custom-designed rug, which was hand-carved to match the elegant details of the table base. To reflect the continental ambience of a European mansion, this interior was elaborately furnished with items drawn from all over the world. The result is a dramatic impression of luxurious formality befitting this Hawaiian mansion."

Jack Adams, Adams Design, Inc.
1415 Kalakaua Avenue, Suite 204, Honolulu, Hawaii 96826
Tel.: (808) 955-6100, Fax: (808) 947-4311

Photography: Ed Espero

Michael Anthony

Specializing in both residential and commercial interior design, Michael Anthony is principal designer and president of Michael Anthony/Associates Interior Design, Inc. in San Francisco. In addition to numerous private residences throughout the United States, Mr. Anthony has designed interiors for the 1150 Sacramento building, the 1700 Van Ness building, the Taldan Architectural Group, and Pacific Presbyterian Medical Center. He was featured as one of 'The Best American Interior Designers' by *House & Garden* in 1988, and was a Guest of the Canadian Government at the 1991 International Interior Design Exposition.

"I wanted to give this living room a design that would be grand yet restrained, imposing but simple. Restraint is evident in the wall paneling, which I had glazed in tones of French putty, and in the uncomplicated elegance of the creamy textured sisal carpet against the dark wood floor. The furniture shapes are at once simple and assertive. Aside from a few well-chosen accessories and the natural marbling of the fireplace, pattern is confined to two striped silk fabrics and the bolder tiger print used on the pillows and stool. Color is realized by the contrasting play of darks against off-whites, brightened by the highlights of gold in the Regency-style mirror and the frame of the Matisse line-lithograph. Richness is achieved through studied simplicity rather than elaborate ornamentation. This design bespeaks my personal perspective on interiors — one that is strongly sculptural, combined with an interest in classical antique pieces and unusual artifacts, such as the encased primitive New Guinea mask and the Tang period Chinese three-legged vessel. Accent pieces, potted plants, and subtle lighting complete this eclectic environment which engages the past in a clearly contemporary dialogue."

Michael Anthony, Michael Anthony Associates.
Sixty-Six Eureka Street, San Francisco, California 94114
Tel.: (415) 255-3066, Fax: (415) 255-9168

Photography: Dennis Anderson

Joseph P. Horan, ASID

*A*fter years of experience as a designer with W&J Sloane, Joseph Horan founded his own firm in 1981. The recipient of numerous awards for his civic and professional activities, Mr. Horan's work has been featured in two design books, *Interior Visions* and *The New Decorating Book*, as well as in newspapers and magazines throughout the United States.

"*B*old color and exaggeration of height create a dramatic flair in this formal guest bedroom. I used ebony for the carpet and ceiling, then a deep pomegranate for the crackle-glazed, strie walls that extend into a coved cornice. A multicolor print was selected for the ceiling-high treatment of the canopy bed, with this floral motif extending to the needlepoint rug. Regency-style balloon shades at the windows permit maximum sunlight exposure during the day, then drop down to provide intimacy and privacy at night."

Joseph P. Horan, Joseph Horan Interior Design
3299 Washington Street, San Francisco, California 94115-1601
Tel.: (415) 346-5646

Photography: John Vaughan

Norma King

Commercial, residential and hospitality interior designer Norma King was born in La Mesa, Texas in 1960. She was educated in interior design at the Fashion and Art Institute of Dallas. Since 1980, she has owned and operated her own interior design firm, and currently has offices in Houston and Athens. Ms. King is a member of both ASID and TAID and has won numerous professional and public awards. She has been a showcase home design participant in Houston, and has designed the interiors of numerous commercial, residential and hospitality projects throughout the United States, Mexico, the south of France, Italy and Greece.

"This large living room is the focal point of a 10,000 square-foot home I designed in Gardendale, Texas. This project gave me the opportunity to create the architectural space planning, the selection of exterior finishes, as well as the extensive landscaping. Although this space is large, I selected minimal design furnishings to respect the room's vast openness. The expansive walls are uncluttered by artwork, thereby placing an emphasis on the large solid oak arched windows which open out to the home's boundless acreage filled with hundreds of quarterhorses. The same dark oak was used for the ceiling, adding warmth to the massive stone and marble fireplace. Throughout the room I used only natural colors and materials such as stone, travertine, oak, *saltillo* tile, suede and natural textiles. Elegant, traditional furnishings and fine bronzes are mixed with very rustic pieces to create an eclectic, livable ambience. Although I now work in various styles on an international level, this room will always be special because it takes me back to my roots in west Texas."

Norma King, Norma King Designz
P.O. Box 980172, Houston, TX 77098   P.O. Box 70043, Glyfada 16610 Athens, Greece
Tel.: (713) 524-1172   *Tel.: (30) 1-984-2039*

Photography: Paola Isola Kapitanakis

Patricia Klee

A designer of commercial, residential and ranch interiors, as well as an architectural designer, Patricia Klee studied at The Buckley School and completed her education at the University of California. Since 1971 she has been the owner of P.K. Design in Santa Barbara. For the past ten years she has also been an associate, design consultant or project coordinator for various companies and firms. Her major projects include the design and development of a commercial retail center in Los Angeles and several ranches and residences in Southern California, throughout the mainland U.S. and Hawaii. Her projects have appeared in numerous publications, including *Ranch and Coast Magazine* and *Design Profiles*.

"*W* ith its thirteen foot ceiling, exposed wooden beams, rough plastered walls, and sixteen sited French doors, this music room and accompanying sunroom presented both luxurious space and architectural character. The interior design is definitely eclectic—over a floor of distressed oak parquetry stained in a terra cotta tone, I spread a dazzling Irish wool area rug. Scattered around the Bechstein grand piano are contemporary Italian suede sofas and slipper chairs, a 19th century sofa and settee covered in cotton velvet, 18th century coromandel side tables, carved Spanish colonial corner tables and chest, French style lounge chairs covered in Laotian silk, and a Venetian mirror. No matter how large the number of guests, the furnishings, placement and style of decoration create an intimate atmosphere and relaxed formality."

Patricia Klee, PK Design
Post Office Box 31150, Santa Barbara, California
Tel.: (805) 687-7894

Photography: James Chen

Pat Larin, ASID

*P*at Larin founded her namesake company in 1980 and has built one of the leading design firms in the San Francisco Bay area. A graduate of Cornell University, she is a Professional Member of ASID. Her projects encompass remodeling and new construction in addition to interior design. As a general contractor, Ms. Larin is able to provide design services from conception to completion. Known for her timeless designs, she is the recipient of many awards and has been elected to *Who's Who in Interior Design*. Ms. Larin has been widely published on the local and national level, including a recent cover for *Better Homes & Gardens*.

"*M*y challenge was to transform an 1800 square-foot room into a personal space. I selected an international style of informal elegance to create a gracious and inviting ambiance. Twelve-foot windows set in alcoves are framed with quilted chintz draperies, but left open to grand vistas. The fresco painting visually lowers the ceiling while the melon glaze gives a warm glow. Chintz, chenille, tapestry and leather in rich jewel tones are accented with interesting fringes, braids and tassels. Cozy, overstuffed chairs and sofas have been arranged in multiple seating areas for a sense of intimacy. The resulting blend of antique and contemporary furnishings, art and accessories creates a timeless space of comfort and drama."

Pat Larin, ASID, Pat Larin Interiors
12720 Dianne Drive, Los Altos Hills, California 94022
Tel.: (415) 941-4613, Fax (415) 941-4047

Photography: John Vaughan

Cheryl K. Monroe, ASID

*S*pecializing in both commercial and residential interiors, Cheryl Monroe has completed numerous office, hotel and restaurant projects, and has designed private residences throughout the United States and Europe. She earned her Bachelor of Arts in Design from the University of Washington, and her Master of Architecture degree from Fountainbleau Academy of Fine Arts. After working in store and commercial design for firms in Beverly Hills and Seattle, she founded Monroe & Company International, Inc. in Bellevue, Washington. Ms. Monroe is a member of the American Society of Interior Designers, the International Council of Shopping Centers and the Seattle Master Builders Association.

"*T*o accommodate my client's requirements for entertaining guests, this design challenged me to create the feeling of a continuous area from two distinct spaces. To enhance the sense of continuity between the areas, I began with the lumination design, selecting the same indirect lighting along with natural wood molding and trim for both spaces. To give the foyer area a somewhat formal atmosphere, I used an elegant hardwood pattern for the flooring of oak and walnut, and placed the 1938 Steinway grand piano as the focal point in this space. The living room was designed in a more casual tone, with conversation by the limestone fireplace in mind. This area is furnished with a pair of matching over-stuffed sofas, placed on either side of a glass-top coffee table. The eight-panel antique lacquered Shoji screen adds a dramatic flair, while the screen's colors are repeated in the fabric of the oversized ottoman. For final accessories, I added plants, bronze and lacquered sofa tables, and a pair of hurricane lamps positioned on the sides of the fireplace. The house was fully renovated on Lake Washington, Bellevue, Washington."

Cheryl K. Monroe, ASID, Monroe & Company International, Inc.
555 108th Northeast, Suite 1, Bellevue, Washington 98004
Tel.: (206) 455-3227, Fax: (206) 455-4098

Photography: Grant Ramaley

Walter Nelson, ASID

*E*ducated at the Rudolph Schaeffer School of Design in San Francisco, Walter Nelson began his interior design career at Cannell & Chaffin Interiors in La Jolla in 1967. He started his own design firm, Nelson Limited, in 1977. Walter Nelson is a member of the Design Curriculum Board at the University of California at San Diego, and served as a professor at San Diego State College for five years. A versatile designer, his work includes contemporary, traditional, deco, and neo-classical styles. He has designed numerous private residences, offices, hotels and restaurants throughout the United States, Canada and Mexico.

"*L*ocated on a ranch, this project called for the transformation of a disused equestrian tack room into a spacious master bedroom. I started by having the pine paneling stripped and bleached to make it as light as possible, and then having the ceiling and casing painted a stark white for tonal contrast. The structural addition of a pair of bookcases was made to frame an existing window and at the same time create a window seat area. For warmth, I carpeted the floor in mohair light pile corduroy, and added a dhurrie area rug to set off the sitting area. The unusual headboard is made from an old discarded iron gate from the ranch. As the final element, I selected the fabrics in varying shades of white, using a variation of textures and patterns to create a discreet but effective visual interest throughout the room."

Walter Nelson, ASID, Nelson Limited
Post Office Box 4130, Leucadia, California 92023
Tel.: (619) 753-9058, Fax: (619) 753-3787

Photography: Harold Davis

104

Photography: Weston Gorin

Penni Paul

*A*fter graduating from Woodbury College with a degree in Interior Design, Penni Paul went on to study at the Chouinard Art Institute and the University of Southern California. She is the owner of Penni Paul Interiors in Beverly Hills, and has been actively involved in the design field for the past twenty-eight years. For fourteen years she instructed classes for the Western Home Furnishings Association, teaching the fundamentals of textiles, color, history of furniture, and general interior design. Ms. Paul has co-produced educational video tapes and has appeared on several television shows in San Diego and Los Angeles. A participant in numerous Pasadena Showcase Houses, Ms. Paul's work has been published in the *Los Angeles Times, Interior Design, House Beautiful, Architectural Digest* and various other publications.

"*E*legance co-existing with relaxing warmth was the key to my design of this entertainment room, situated in a West Los Angeles penthouse. I began this design around the built-in media center – which is the focal point of the room – containing a mixed display of books, photographs and fine art objects. For the room's main seating, I selected a large circular sofa covered in deep green leather, accented by a multi-colored Oriental rug in which greens and flamingo prevail.

"*T*he sense of warm refinement extends to the walls, which I had hand-glazed in greens and bronze. The soft folds of the Roman shades complement the color scheme, while the coffered ceiling adds depth and architectural interest. I selected cove lighting to add a soft brightness to the room's overall depth of tone. The ornate glass-top cocktail table serves as a balance to the softness of the sofa and the more austere lines of the media center.

"*A*lthough I used green as a primary color in this room, the overall tonal effect comes from the play of glossy black moldings and cabinet supports against the satin sheen of pale woods in the cabinet facings and floor. The result is a somewhat Asian simplicity. This design stresses the horizontal lines, complements the larger art objects and creates the calming influence this room was meant to have."

Penni Paul, Penni Paul Interiors
170 South Beverly Drive, Beverly Hills, California 90212
Tel.: (310) 276-8005, Fax: (310) 276-8908

Jenny Real-Ortiz

*A*fter obtaining her Bachelor of Arts in Interior Design, Jenny Real-Ortiz opened her business in 1974. Her innovative designs and flair for bold use of natural material brought her national acclaim. Her business is centered in Mexico City where she offers a complete range of decorating and architectural assessment services, as well as custom-designed furniture.

"*M*y client's instructions, 'make a statement in color and form', made the design of this living/dining room in Mexico City a wonderfully creative experience. Wanting original designs and a bold look, my client provided photographs of favorite sculptures from various museums to offer a vision for this room's design. I based my designs on these art forms, and actually incorporated these pictures into the decor. Bright colors and geometric shapes give the illusion of expanded space and offer an invitation to interact with the room. I designed the dining chairs with curves in the lower half – edged in red – and sharp angles edged in bright yellow for the upper portions. Royal blue fabric covers the seats, supported by traditional legs painted in a sharply contrasting jet-black. The same bright primary colors and geometric shapes are carried on through the living area. The total effect is a bold artistic expression, creating the exciting and unique setting my client desired."

Jenny Real-Ortiz, Telas Ideas y Proyectos, S.A. de C.V.
Monte Libano 255, Lomas de Chapultepec, Mexico City PC11000, Mexico
Tel.: (52) 5-540-20-53, Fax: (52) 5-202-61-70

Photography: Angela Caparroso

109

Gloria Roberts, ISID

*G*loria Roberts was educated at Riverside Business College, the University of Southern California and Harvard School of Design. She began her career in 1958 as an assistant designer with Irving Komorrow Interiors. In 1966, she took a position as an interior designer with Binfords. Since 1979, she has been Owner and Principal Designer of Gloria Balogh Interiors; she is married to Gaylor Wilson Singletary.

*I*n addition to being a featured speaker on radio shows and at various service clubs, Ms. Roberts has taught classes in Interior Design at Riverside Community College, Loma Linda University, and for the schools of John Robert Powers. An active member of the International Society of Interior Designers, the Riverside Art Museum, and the Riverside Art Alliance, she is also a past president and charter member of the Assistance League of Riverside. Since 1970, Ms. Roberts has been a participating designer for numerous Showcase Houses, including Edgemont in 1982, Poppy Hill in 1984, and Casa Arroyo in 1986.

*G*loria Roberts' major projects include the conference room and president's office of Riverside Community College, and the Administration Building and University House of the University of California at Riverside, which she completed in 1990. Ms. Roberts' work has been featured in numerous publications, including *House & Garden, House Beautiful, Better Homes & Gardens, Designers West, Interiors, Inland Empire Magazine,* and the *Los Angeles Times.*

"*I* call my favorite room *Comedor Romantico.* This dining room's tranquil atmosphere is created by the soft muted pastel colorings and elegant Mediterranean furnishings. Both the window treatments and the textured walls are accented by a custom-designed Oriental rug. The richly appointed table settings of fine china, sparkling crystal and gleaming silver glow warmly in the old world tradition beneath a beautiful chandelier. This room's magnificence is personalized by exquisite details, such as the hand-painted ceiling design and hand-painted wall mural. I added carefully chosen antique accessories and selected luxurious upholstery to complement the room's motif.

"*F*lowers, I decided, would be the room's signature, since they naturally embrace the theme of romance. I repeated the design from the arm chairs on the window valance, and the flowers on the ceiling are repeated in the mural. Flower arrangements adorn both the dining table and the side table centered in the window. The idyllic view of the garden completes the romantic aura, suitable for entertaining in the grand manner but without stiffness or cold formality."

Gloria Roberts, ISID, Gloria Balogh Interiors
1733 Massachusetts Avenue, Riverside, California 92507
Tel.: (909) 787-9279, Fax: (909) 683-7291

Photography: David Valenzuela

Judy Robins

*S*ince establishing her residential interior design practice in 1975, Judy Robins has completed projects in Denver, as well as in New York, Beverly Hills, Aspen and Vail. In addition to her eighteen years as an interior designer, and art consultant, Judy has served as a trustee for the Denver Art Museum since 1986 and has taught Interior Design at Metropolitan State College.

"*I* wanted to create a dramatic yet understated ambience for this Denver living room. In order to invoke a feeling of both sophistication and comfort, I chose colors of mushroom, putty, creams and black as a subtle complement to the luxurious materials of silk, limestone, chinoiserie and marble. I also wanted to incorporate the client's beautiful collection of antique Asian artifacts, which I featured in a custom-designed vitrine. To complete this design, I added inset ceiling lights around the entire perimeter of the room and window alcove area."

Judy Robins, Judy Robins Interiors
755 Lafayette Street, Denver, Colorado 80218
Tel.: (303) 832-3265, Fax: (303) 830-6939

Photography: Don Riley

114

Mary Sorenson

Mary Sorenson launched Cedar Hill Design, Inc. in 1983, with offices located in Cedar Hill's historic downtown. Her major projects include numerous private residences, as well as Western Bank, Lakeview Community Church, and the Cedar Hill Chamber of Commerce building.

"The client's request appeared straightforward: to assist the coordination of their remodeling and home addition project. The architect had designated this room – once the garage – as a piano room. An analysis of the floorplan, however, indicated that there were several unanswered questions: where will the clients' place their massive collection of books, where will they sit to write their next book, where will they have their jam sessions? To solve these daily living problems, I began this design by ringing the walls with library shelves – including a computer center – thereby bringing everything close at hand to compose a song or write a book. The opposite walls were lined with French doors and windows, leading to the living and conversation areas. This space allows the accommodation of groups of thirty people or intimacy for two, all of whom can enjoy the lake and piney woods view. Our concept is to always create something both wonderful to look at, and even more wonderful to live with."

Mary Sorenson, Cedar Hill Design Center, Inc.
712 Cedar Street, Cedar Hill, Texas 75104
Tel.: (214) 291-2070, Fax: (214) 293-0378

Photography: Jack Weigler

Edward Turrentine, ASID

Southern California designer Edward Turrentine received his Bachelor of Arts degree from Woodbury University, where he currently serves on the Board of Trustees. After designing for Ashburns Furniture Co., John White Interiors, Mayco Stores of California and Candlelight Interiors, he founded Edward C. Turrentine Interior Design, Inc. in 1971. He specializes both in residential and commercial design, his projects spanning the country from California to Maine. Mr. Turrentine is a member of the American Society of Interior Designers, and received the IF/ASID Outstanding Residential Designer Award for 1988-1989 and 1990-1991. He has appeared on a number of television features and his work has graced the covers of numerous design publications including *House Beautiful, House and Garden, Los Angeles Homes,* and *Designers West.*

"I designed this grand Pavilion to accentuate and complement the original architecture of the Wallace Neff Estate. This addition had to be carefully planned and supervised to adhere to the time-quality of the original Mediterranean estate. I added textured walls, glazed to resemble old Italianate stone. Accordingly, the accent colors within the room were confined to a muted palette, allowing the rich details of the antique furnishings to speak for themselves. The grand salon which connects to this Pavilion, on the other hand, has a very warm, golden glow. Small conversational areas abound, featuring a pair of chairs set *tête-a-tête* fashion on either side of a pedestaled statue of a lyrist. Rich window and floor treatments enhance the large antique pieces. This design emphasizes my philosophy that architectural backgrounds, the client's tastes, and attention to detail are co-equal elements of good design."

Edward Turrentine, ASID, Edward C. Turrentine Interior Design, Inc.
70 North Raymond Avenue, Pasadena, California 91103
Tel.: (818) 795-9964, Fax: (818) 795-0027

Photography: Jeremy Samuelson

116

Carol Wharton, ISID

Since 1978, Carol Wharton has been the owner and interior design director of Carol Wharton & Associates in Redondo Beach, California. A Long Beach native, she attended the University of California at Los Angeles. Early in her career she was the first director of design for the LCM Hospital Design Show House. Ms. Wharton has served on the Palos Verdes Chamber of Commerce, and was named Woman of the Month by *Flair* magazine.

In addition to the home of actor Tom Sullivan, Ms. Wharton's major projects have included many California residences in Rolling Hills, Rancho Palos Verdes and Lake Arrowhead. Numerous office and commercial projects, such as the showroom for Whittlesey Motors' Jaguar showroom in Torrance, are also listed among her credits. Since 1980, Ms. Wharton's work has been widely published, most recently in the *Los Angeles Times, South Bay Living, Home & Garden, Palos Verdes Review, Designers West*, and *Architectural Digest*.

"The greatest asset of this hilltop living room in Rolling Hills Estates also posed its chief design challenge: how to incorporate its fabulous exterior view into the interior design scheme without one element overshadowing the other. The profusion of treetops and light, combined with the vaulted beamed ceilings seemed to make a sophisticated provincial approach a natural. Crisp white walls and ceilings give the room spaciousness and open it up to the outdoors, counterpointed by the dark wood tones of the furniture, hall paneling and exterior trim.

"Lacey white scalloped sheers soften the ceiling line and the expanses of glass, while taking full advantage of the dramatic landscape. A light-grounded floral motif dominates the pair of chairs and area rug, with the chair upholstery repeated in the curtain trim and tiebacks. The salmon color of the matching sofas' geometric fabric takes its cue from a shade common to the rug and chairs, adding bright drama to the room. The collection of fine blue and white china also repeats a shade found in the floral patterns, and it seems to bring the vast blue sky into the room as a design element. Similarly, a liberal use of indoor greenery blends into the treescape beyond.

"The play of dark woods against bright fabrics, formal against informal pieces – the silver tea set and the ruffled windowpane throw pillows – lends the room a certain delicacy despite the large proportions of the furnishings. The room has definite substance, while still maintaining an illusion that it practically floats above the city below."

Carol Wharton, ISID, Carol Wharton & Associates, Inc.
221 Avenida del Norte, Redondo Beach, California 90277
Tel.: (310) 540-5058

Photography: David Valenzuela

Barbara Woolf, ISID

*B*arbara Woolf studied Art and Interior Design at UCLA, and founded her interior design firm in 1966. Her work has been published in *Designers West, The Designer, Today's Living,* and numerous editions of *The Los Angeles Times Homes Magazine.* Barbara Woolf's major projects include the Pickfair Mansion, the executive offices of The Los Angeles Forum, the Sunset Towers Hotel as well as numerous private residences throughout California and Hawaii.

"*T*his 'Russian Red Living Room' challenged me to create an exciting atmosphere while working with a relatively small space. I selected a strong red background color as the room's unifying element, and then incorporated numerous exotic accessories into the design. I designed the loft to serve for overflow during parties and to double as a guest room; I gave this area a Middle Eastern motif to accent the main room below. Finally, I extended the atmosphere of the living room out into both the dining area and the outdoor patio to create enough space to allow for entertaining up to seventy people in this Beverly Hill maisonette."

Barbara Woolf, ISID, Barbara Woolf Interiors, Inc.
120 South Robertson Boulevard, Los Angeles, California 90048
Tel.: (310) 859-1970, Fax: (310) 278-3530

Photography: George Szanik

INTERNATIONAL RESIDENTIAL DESIGN

Countess Monika Apponyi, Showcase Bedroom, London

Cristina Bertolazzi, Grand Salon, Sao Paulo

Gloria Bordaberry Boxer, Seaside Living/Dining Room, Uruguay

Vicki Grace, FCSD, Colonial Living Room, Kuala Lumpur

Lisbeth Mathisen Grundt, Norwegian Dining Room, Oslo

Leonardo Junqueira, Formal Living Room, Sao Paulo

Richard H. Klein, BSID, Terrace Living Room, Bermuda

Ricardo Mayer, ASID, Copacabana Dining Room, Rio de Janeiro

Yoshiko Mononobe, Modern Japanese Dining Room, Tokyo

Kevin Patrick Mullarkey, MIDDA, Young Lady's Bedroom, Galway

Wajih Naccache, Penthouse Entry/Salon, United Arab Emirates

Prem Nath, ASID, Rajasthan Bedroom, Bombay

Alberto Pinto, Columned Entry/Grand Salon, Paris

Leticia Chaves Ray, Contemporary Solarium, Paraguay

Jacqueline Thwaites, ISID, Traditional Living Room, London

John Wilman, Farmhouse Dining Room, Lancashire

*Overlooking the fountain in Sharjah Lagoon in the United Arab Emirates,
this penthouse master bedroom offers a refined but soothing elegance.
Interior design: Wajih Naccache. Photography: Robert Emmett Bright.*

Photography: Gavin Kingcome

Countess Monika Apponyi

*P*ride and professionalism motivate Monika Apponyi to reflect the preferences and tastes of her clients, while she infuses into each project her own flair for richly comfortable interiors. Countess Apponyi was born and raised in Austria, and came to the United Kingdom for her studies, where she graduated from the Inchbald School in 1978. The two years following her graduation saw commissions from a number of private patrons in London for both houses and apartments. Her commercial clients included Pepsi Cola and the fabric showrooms of Pallu and Lake. Her projects have been published in *House & Gardens* and *House & Gardens Kitchens and Bathrooms*.

*M*arriage and family commitments took Countess Apponyi to Frankfurt in 1981, where she and a partner established MM Designs. Immediate success followed as they undertook refurbishment of the guest house for the Deutsche Bundesbank, branches of the First National Bank of Boston in Germany and Luxembourg, and 120 rooms of the Hotel Bristol in Paris. With her return to London in 1985, the independent London branch of MM Design has established itself as a premiere design firm, through which she enjoys commissions from all over Europe. Her willingness to develop a variety of styles has won her a loyal patronage of clients. While new clients continue to be attracted to Countess Apponyi's designs, her real business strength is based firmly on her record for strict accountability and close attention to detail at every stage.

"I ventured into a new style when designing this guest room. I wanted a simplistic feeling of elegance and warmth, without being over-decorated or over-furnished. Light spaciousness was my goal in creating a room that would endear itself to any visitor. My predominant color was white, including the bed-hangings, curtains, and walls, muted by fabrics which softened the effect and eliminated any threat of starkness. I then decided upon blue for the secondary color before selecting fabrics from Ralph Lauren's 'Morgan Hall' collection. The blue accents in the bed linen and the seats of the side chairs is carried over into the band of blue outlining each wall at the ceiling.

*"M*odern lighting allowed me to create interesting pools of brilliance and shade that enhanced the room's ambience. Spot lighting on the ceiling accented the art work and floor-to-ceiling bed-hangings and curtains. Strategically-placed occasional lamps then provided overall room lighting for function and utility. The result is a bright, summery quality, combined with a visual freshness produced by the white and blue color theme. The remainder of the furnishings and accessories were chosen for their ability to blend classical elegance with intimate simplicity. The result is at once impressive and infinitely relaxing."

Countess Monika Apponyi, MCSD, IDDA, FISID, MM Design
16 South Terrace, London SW7 2TD, England
Tel.: (44) 71-584-7267, Fax: (44) 71-823-8288

Cristina Bertolazzi

*R*esidential interior design projects are the specialty of Cristina Bertolazzi, partner in the firm of Piani and Disegni, based in Sao Paulo, Brazil. She co-founded the company in the 1980's, to which she brought her talents and expertise as its principal interior designer. Ms. Bertolazzi has completed interior design assignments for town-houses, country estates, apartments and offices. Her primary objective in every commission is to reflect the aspirations and personalities of each client individually, and she approaches her projects with this perspective in mind.

"*T*he feeling of intimacy was my goal for this grand Sao Paulo living room, where I needed to combine a contemporary interpretation of classical style with a view toward Brazilian culture. As a starting point, I chose two L-shaped sofas to surround the elegant fireplace and mantel, the room's undisputed focal point. Rich draperies – in the same pale beige as the sofas – dress the large windows. I then chose terracotta vases and antique African cushions for color accents. Art pieces, including a bronze representing an Indian, introduce the Brazilian touch within the room's classical elements, giving a unique identity to this traditionally styled home."

Cristina Bertolazzi, Piani & Disegni, Arquitetura e Interiores
Rua da Consolacoa, 3407 Casa 6, Sao Paulo, Brazil
Tel.: (55) 11-280-7011, Fax: (55) 11-280-7578

Photography: Alain Brugier

127

Gloria Bordaberry Boxer

*A*fter completing her studies in Uruguay's capital city of Montevideo, Gloria Bordaberry Boxer began her career as an interior designer at Moncalvo's Institute. Presently a designer for the Carlos and Jaime Boxer Anaya Studio, her major projects include the interior design of numerous summer homes in the seaside community of Punta del Este. Ms. Boxer has designed many commercial projects for retail shops and offices in addition to her specialty of seaside villas and country homes. Her commercial interior design projects include the director's office for Calvin Klein in Argentina and the president's office for the Bank of Santander in Carrasco.

"*W*ith its spectacular view of Portezuelo Bay in Punta del Este, I wanted to bring the feeling of the water, the seaside and the sunset into this room. I began by adding character to the room's architecture, using beams from an old wooden quai from the seashore to frame the fireplace and accent the walls. For fabric and paint colors, I selected sea greens and blues, set off with pale pinks. As soft light pours in from outside and washes over the stone floor, 18th century elements, Chinese pottery, potted palms, brass accessories, and handmade rattan furniture coexist in harmony, all bathed in the timeless calm of the natural environment."

Gloria Bordaberry Boxer, Interior Designer
Ing. Luis Andreoni 7210, Carrasco-Montevideo, Uruguay
Tel.: (598) 2-60-17-02, Fax: (598) 2-60-35-40

Photography: Jorge Köhli

129

Vicki Grace, FCSD

Australian-born Vicki Grace was educated at Sydney University and the London College of Furniture, and is a Fellow of the Chartered Society of Designers. Ms. Grace is currently Managing Director of Addison Marc Sdn. Bhd. in Malaysia. She has designed interiors for boutiques, galleries, corporate offices, hotels and exhibitions throughout England, Kuala Lumpur and Singapore, as well as in Penang and Saudi Arabia.

"Set inside a vintage black-and-white colonial house in Malaysia, I designed this living room to be a serene haven to retire to in the evenings. Aside from the two vases of Oriental orchids, the room is devoid of any intense color. I allowed the changing hues of light filtering through slatted screens and adjoining balconies to function in lieu of bright paint or dye as the chief tonal interest in the room. The interplay of natural materials also functions in this way. Bustling with colonial charm, the natural light illuminates the crumbling plaster and the antiquated electrical wiring which snakes down the walls. For contrast of tone, I selected pale wall colors and upholstered pieces to juxtapose with the natural wood tables and flooring. The intricately carved center table – actually a Thai opium bed – is set off by the simplicity of the disconnected sectional seating around it. The exotic figures of the Burmese dancers are foiled by the sleek Japanese kimono stand and the Chinese porcelain pieces. The uncluttered simplicity of this graceful space provides the ideal refuge I wanted to create."

Vicki Grace, FCSD, Addison Marc (M) Sdn Bhd
7 Jalan Kia Peng, Kuala Lumpur 50450, Malaysia
Tel.: (60) 3-248-2100, Fax: (60) 3-248-2164

Lisbeth Grundt

Oslo-based designer Lisbeth Grundt conducted her interior design studies at the Colorado Institute of Art and Loretto Heights College in the United States. She began her career as a kitchen designer with the firm of Huseby & Son, Vale, Vestfold in 1971, and later became a staff designer with Interdesign. After gaining thirteen years of interior design experience, she founded Design Concept in Oslo, Norway, in 1984. Ms. Grundt specializes in both residential and contract work, including hotel and restaurant design. Among her major projects are renovation work for Thomas Hefteyagt, interior design for Fyresdal Turishotel, Telemark, the University of Oslo, Kjobmandsbanken, and Alfred Berg Marine. Lisbeth Grundt's work has been published in *A-Magasinet*, *Byggeindustrien*, and *Byggenytt*.

"In creating the design for this room, I had to keep in mind that it would serve three functions: living room, dining room and library. The client had moved from a 19th-century apartment to this Swiss chalet-style house, and I needed to create a setting that would match the ambience of the house while utilizing the furniture from the previous residence.

"I began this design by selecting a Lelievre chintz as drapery fabric for the wall-length windows. This fabric was repeated on the armchairs in order to create a natural transition between the activity centers of the room. The large, Arteluce chandelier suspended from the vaulted ceiling acted to balance the glass-top table with brass and chrome base. To create a focal point for the living room and dining room areas, I designed a new fireplace, complete with custom brass trimmings.

"Within the dining area itself, I had Swedish reproductions of old Empire chairs covered in multicolored fabric. I then used a large area rug to enhance the warmth of both the wood ceiling paneling and the refurbished oak parquet floor. The walls were stripped of a textile wall covering and recovered in a striped, slightly shiny wallpaper from JAB. To accentuate the height and natural elegance of the room, I used numerous plants and floral arrangements throughout the space. As final accents, I had paintings hung on either side of the china cabinet, and embellished the dining table with candelabras and formal place settings."

Lisbeth Mathisen Grundt, Design Concept
Uranienborg Terr. 10, Oslo, Norway 0351
Tel.: (47) 22-46-56-23, Fax: (47) 22-64-03-04

133

Leonardo Junqueira

*A*fter a three year apprenticeship as a design company overseer, Leonardo Junqueira formed a partnership with interior designer Cristina Bertolazzi to start their own design firm in Sao Paulo. Their architectural and interior designs can be seen in town and country houses, apartments and offices throughout Brazil, each created with a classical perspective that ranges from a minimalist styling to the luxuriously opulent.

"*I* achieved my favorite modern interpretation of classical style in the salon of this Sao Paulo residence. Facing the fireplace, two contemporary sofas are arranged against pale beige curtains and accented with an antique French rococo console. The Manabu Mabe canvas dramatizes and reflects the colorful modern accents in the room, while antiques and various accessories were each chosen to add a sense of classical comfort. As final elegant details, a delicate sculpture, a porcelain vessel and a fine blue crystal lamp were selected to grace the antique French marbletop sidetable."

Leonardo Junqueira, Piani & Disegni Arquitetura e Interiores
Rue da Consolacao, 3407 Casa 6, Sao Paulo, SP, Brazil 01416001
Tel.: (55) 11-280-7011, Fax.: (55) 11-280-7578

Photography: Alain Brugier

134

Richard H. Klein

*R*ichard Klein graduated from Dartmouth College and received a Master of Fine Arts Degree from Yale. He worked at Labalme Associates and CNI International in New York, where he also worked on the design of 'Maxwell's Plum' with the restaurateur, Warner Leroy. He jointly formed the interior design group, Hamma Galleries in Bermuda, in 1972. His projects include corporate offices for Gulf Oil and Bacardi International; retail shops, small hotels and residences in Bermuda, New York, Dallas, Palm Beach and Mustique.

*R*ichard Klein's work balances his clients' requirements, the architectural elements of the site and the salient classic principles of proportion, scale, color and detail. Designer and clients share an appreciation of quality materials that contributes to comfortable, personal, and effective rooms.

"*T*his house sits on the southern edge of Bermuda's Great Sound and the living room opens to a broad terrace through wide pocket doors. As a foil to the dramatic, colorful and unique setting, we chose traditional detailing with natural, endemic materials to create a calm background for the bold profiles of selected antiques and contemporary art: a hand carved Bermuda limestone fireplace surround; a prized, early 18th century Bermuda cedar tea table; McGuire lounge chairs and ottomans with fabrics by Fortuny and Canovas; a 1920's English pond yacht and bronzes by Bruno Romeda stand out against this sun-drenched room. A lush tropical garden beyond contrasts the simplicity of the interiors."

Richard H. Klein, BSID, Hamma Galleries
One Lane Hill, Hamilton, Bermuda
Tel.: (809) 292-8500, Fax: (809) 292-8424

Photography: Ann Spurling

Ricardo Mayer, ASID

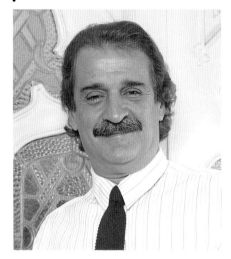

Born in Rio de Janeiro, Ricardo Mayer applies his knowledge of architecture and interior design to each of his commercial, retail and residential projects. Mr. Mayer studied at the Instituto La Fayette and National University before establishing his architectural firm in 1970. He is a Professional Member of the American Society of Interior Designers, as well as a member of the Cooper-Hewitt Museum in New York, and the National Trust for Historic Preservation.

"**L**ight colors and carefully executed plaster details on the ceiling and door framing were two techniques I used to mask the cubic structure of this apartment on Copacabana Beach. The use of recessed lighting enhances this soft coloring and gives a free movement between the room's spaces. I chose muted fabrics and colors for the upholstery, while allowing the paintings and sculpture to draw the viewer from piece to piece by their varied textures and design. The matched vases and table runner add an elegant, traditional touch to the glass and marble-based dining table. To further escape the architectural constraints of the shape of the room, I used a liberal number of Oriental rugs throughout the entire space."

Ricardo Mayer, ASID, Arquitetura e Planejamento
680-708 Avenida Copacabana, Rio de Janeiro, Brazil 22050
Tel.: (55) 21-256-8616, Fax: (55) 21-256-8616

Photography: Juca Moraes

Yoshiko Mononobe

*H*aving studied interior design in Europe, the United States and the former Soviet Union, Yoshiko Mononobe works primarily on the residences and summer homes of top Japanese industrialists, entrepreneurs, corporate executives and celebrities. She is Executive President of AIAP Interior Design in Tokyo, and is a Professional Member of the Japan Interior Designers Association. Ms. Mononobe has been listed in three editions of *Who's Who in Interior Design*.

"*I* wanted this dining room to reflect the gracious spirit of receiving and serving cherished and important guests. To soften and expand the surrounding space, I applied light pastel cloth wallcovering to the ceiling and walls. To further this effect, a similarly pale-toned carpet was laid over the floor. The built-in cabinet and shelving are designed to be both functional and beautiful. The horizontal beams which span them add a sense of intimacy in contrast to the high ceiling. Again in the interest of functionality, the cabinet in the foreground is mobile.

"*T*he simple, elegant dining table is made of rosewood, which harmonizes beautifully with the eight Italian-made chairs. Except for the jewel-toned chair seats, color is stated solely by the various woods used. Nature provides the only pattern: the darks and lights of the table top and the inherent striping in the cabinetry. I chose all of the furniture for its superb quality and graceful styling. The understated pendant lamp above the table, for example, is the room's only obtrusive source of illumination, all other lighting being recessed.

"*T*he room is quietly dramatic, reflecting the good taste of the hosts and guests as well as the elements of truth, goodness and beauty which I believe are the essence of creativity. When it was completed, I felt the combination of elements gave the design refinement, warmth, and stateliness. There is a clean, utilitarian quality proper for an eating place, and yet the room looks inviting. One suspects that the food served at this table will be of gourmet quality, and that the conversation around it will be alive with laughter."

Yoshiko Mononobe, AIAP Interior Design
3-11-8-1206 Setagaya, Setagaya-ku, Tokyo, Japan
Tel.: (81) 3-3426-5057, Fax: (81) 3-5450-1275

Photography: Misso Kawakami

Kevin Mullarkey, MIDDA

As Managing Director of Cotton Box Interiors in Galway, Ireland, Kevin has worked on a variety of refurbishment projects ranging from the Gaiety Theatre Dublin to the Department of Defense to the Pope John Paul Centre. His work has been recognized by the Irish Goods Council and the London Guild.

"Limited interior space and poor natural lighting were the obstacles to overcome in this 'Young Lady's Apartment' in Galway. The solution was to inject bright, vibrant colors, and add numerous lighting sources. The window was screened with pleated gauze in order to obstruct the view of an adjacent building without the loss of light. I chose London's Designer Guild fabrics, Zoffany wallpaper and a sisal floor covering from India to create a spacious and cheerful atmosphere in 498 square feet of space."

Kevin Patrick Mullarkey, MIDDA, Cotton Box Interiors
21 Middle Street, Galway, Ireland
Tel.: (353) 91-64373, Fax: (353) 91-64383

Photography: Neil Warner

143

Wajih Naccache

*F*luent in Arabic, French, Italian and English, Wajih Naccache is a designer on a truly international scale. He began his education at the Beaux Arts in Beirut, where he received a Bachelor's degree in Architecture. He continued his studies in Florence at the University Institute Bell Arts. Mr. Naccache relishes working on the "whole project," an entire house or estate, where he can create a total environment befitting each client's personality and tastes. He has designed the interiors of numerous luxurious homes throughout the Middle East, Europe and other areas of the world.

"*D*esigned for entertaining, this salon was arranged for both large and intimate gatherings in mind. The room itself is spacious and bright, so I enhanced both attributes with a floor-to-ceiling mirror, dramatically accented with a pair of *faux* marble columns. This palatial focal point reflects all aspects of the room, particularly the beautiful travertin floor, which is accented with a rare matched set of Tabriz carpets. The armchairs, flanking the sofa of my own design, are covered in yellow striped satin to complement the yellow silk draperies. To accentuate the elegant charm of the salon, I carried this bright and airy theme into the entrance hall, where I used the same lemon yellow for the sofa and side chairs which are centered in the hall. Thus, the entrance becomes an extension of the salon in welcoming friends and guests – inviting them to relax and enjoy the comfortable, warm ambience created just for them."

Wajih Naccache, Design Team
Naser Street, P.O. Box 1776, Sharjah, United Arab Emirates
Tel.: (971) 6-593035, Fax: (971) 6-597521, Tlx.: 68230 EM

Photography: Robert Emmett Bright

Prem Nath

Commercial interior designer Prem Nath was born in Lyalpur, India in 1941, and received his Architecture Degree from the Sir J.J. College of Architecture in 1965. Mr. Nath has won numerous awards for his design work, including the Hospital Design Competition and the V.K. Patil Foundation Design Competition; in 1980 he was named Outstanding Young Architect by Jaycee International. He has been president of Prem Nath & Associates in Bombay since 1965, and chairman of Prem Nath Consultants Pvt. Ltd. since 1975. Mr. Nath's major projects include the interior design of the Iskon Temple, the five-star Hotel Vasent Continental and film star homes at Bombay, including the celebrity home of Hindujas, the richest Indian family in the world.

"My aim for the decor of this Rajasthan-style bedroom was to capture the rich heritage of Indian maharajas and princes, combined with contemporary subtle tones and modern comforts. I established this theme by designing the sitting area to represent a traditional Indian lounge corner. I selected a low-carved chair and bolster-cushioned divan for this area, and had both upholstered in silk. This is accented with the pastel shades of both the Indian silk bedcover and the marble-lined walls. The miniature painting, the chess table and the enamel and goldleaf wall panels denote the preference for handcrafted native art held by well-to-do Indians who, though modern, are deeply rooted in tradition."

Prem Nath, ASID, Prem Nath & Associates
4, Merewether Road, Apollo Bunder, Bombay 400 039, India
Tel.: (91) 22-202-0029, Fax: (91) 22-287-5150

Photography: Vivek Das

Alberto Pinto

During his twenty years as a designer, Alberto Pinto has created the interiors of apartments, residences, yachts, offices and hotels throughout the world. Mr. Pinto's major accomplishments include the interior design of two cruise ships, Club Med I and Club Med II, and Club Mediterranean facilities in Agadir, Eilat, Guadeloupe, Opio, and Villars Sur Ollon in Switzerland.

"Styled after a Russian palace, this entrance hall features high ceilings and a dramatic pillared doorway. I selected 19th century Aubusson rugs to complement the colors of the mahogany framework, and used matching Italian benches covered in black and green damask as a contrast to the white and black marble floor. Stepping through the doorway, the viewer's focus is drawn to the grandeur of the chandelier and the neoclassical draperies. A series of ten Napolitan *gouaches* paintings continue to emphasize the room's height as they frame the floor-to-ceiling window. I chose a warm color palette to keep the hall bright and cheerful, selecting rose for the armchairs, and peach for the wall coverings and draperies. These colors are also echoed in the rug covering the parquet floor. As a final majestic touch, candelabras and a large flower arrangement were placed on the main table, creating an elegant balance with the chandelier above."

Alberto Pinto, Cabinet Alberto Pinto
61 Quai d'Orsay, Paris 75007, France
Tel.: (33) 1-45-51-03-33, Fax: (33) 1-45-55-51-41

Photography: Giorgio Baroni (room), Roland Beauffre (portrait).

149

Leticia Chaves Ray

*A*lthough her preference lies in residential design and restoration, Leticia Chaves Ray is equally comfortable working with commercial projects including banks, bistros, apartment buildings and corporate offices. She and her staff usually work on eight to ten major projects a year throughout her native Paraguay, and her talents have been sought out by clients in Argentina and Uruguay, as well. In addition to her interior design talents, she is also a decorative painter. Ms. Ray graduated with a degree in Interior Design, obtained her professional interior design license, and has operated her own design studio in Asuncion, Paraguay since 1985.

"*I* wanted to bring a refined character to the solarium of this Paraguayan home, accenting the room without sacrificing its natural serenity and brightness. I started by using a trellis to separate the room from the adjoining breakfast room, thus bringing a certain privacy to this romantic setting. For the room's furnishings, I used antiques combined with pale plaids and florals. The rattan loveseat, rocker and table are late Victorian, while the armchairs, desk and table are French provincial. I painted a glossy pale-blue and white checkerboard pattern on some of these pieces, to contrast with the flat French wash base color. I introduced pastel pinks in the cotton-and-silk dhurrie rug and the striped wallpaper and floral upholstery fabric from Laura Ashley. The lamps on either side of the sofa are my own design. The Ysanne Gayet painting above the fireplace completes this room, depicting the 'August Blossom', a flower found throughout this area of Paraguay."

Leticia Chaves Ray, Leticia Ray Interior Design
Mariscal Estigarribia 1636, Asuncion, Paraguay
Tel.: (595) 21-200-612, Fax: (595) 21-210-846

Photography: Oscar Ynsfrán

Jacqueline Thwaites

*R*eknowned as the principal of the world-famous Inchbald School of Design in London, Mrs. Jacqueline Thwaites was educated at the Convent of the Sacred Heart and the House of Citizenship. In 1960, she founded the Inchbald School where she continues to teach and practice her art. Mrs. Thwaites is a Professional Member of the International Society of Interior Designers, and her work has been published in the *Directory of Interior Designers*, *Bedrooms* and *Design & Decoration*.

"*T*he drawing room of this London apartment is small, but fortunately features a large window which allows plenty of light. To expand both the sunniness and the room's dimensions I began by covering the walls in a pale lemon silk. This coloring continues onto the carpet which is a custom-made Brussels weave. The *Directoire*-style window treatment employs taffeta, again, to a cheerful and sophisticated effect. For furniture emphasis I chose Charles X, in classic designs and pale woods, along with one or two modern pieces. Floral and solid green upholsteries relieve the yellow and bolster the spring-toned palette. For contrast, the dark-hearthed fireplace is punctuated by the iron coffee table base and the silk velvet covering a pair of fine Victorian salon chairs. Their gilded embellishments pick up the golds found in the plant table, drapery fringe, picture frames and the elaborate mirror hanging above the mantle. A profusion of plants and fresh flowers enhances the bright atmosphere that gives this room, though not large, its sunny disposition."

Jacqueline Thwaites, Inchbald School of Design
32 Eccleston Square, London, England SWIV 1PB
Tel.: (44) 71-630-9011, Fax: (44) 71-976-5979

John Wilman

Born in Lancashire, John Wilman studied textile design at the Manchester Regional College of Art. He has won numerous awards for his adaptations of Parisian designs for the contemporary British market. Joining the Reed Paper Group in 1967, he worked in the Crown studio for ten years before moving to Coloroll's Wallcoverings. He headed up the design team that launched Coloroll into the home fashion market under its own name. John Wilman's Shalimar concept of lighting, ceramics, carpets, beds, and upholstered furniture, designed in 1987, rapidly became one of Coloroll's most successful collections. In 1990, with partner Eric Kilby he founded his own company, which currently offers six designer collections under the John Wilman Fabrics and Wallpapers brand name.

"**F**or the dining room of this 17th century farmhouse, I wanted to avoid creating a typical English farmhouse effect. Instead, I featured art decor items such as the glass table, palms, modern paintings and other more contemporary accent pieces. In contrast, I chose traditional fabrics for the draperies and upholstery, which blend well with the 17th century mullion windows and complement the architecture of this traditional English farmhouse. The result is a pleasant, modern atmosphere that remains warm and comfortable."

John Wilman, John Wilman Limited
Riverside Mills, Crawford Street, Nelson Lancashire, England BB9 7QT
Tel.: (44) 282-617-777, Fax.: (44) 282-614-222

Photography: Mark Wilman

WORLDWIDE CONTRACT DESIGN

Roberto Alcantara, Modern Executive Office, Mexico City

Sinee Amoradhat, Convention Center Restaurant, Bangkok

Katherine Bacon, New Brunswick Bell, Canada

Ernesto Francisco Bedmar, Kimin Collection Gallery, Singapore

Consuelo Boom, Furniture Showroom, Mexico City

Moon-Young Choi, CitiGold, Seoul

Solichin Gunawan, Sahid Jaya Hotel's Puri Agung Hall, Jakarta

Masae Kawamura, Main Restaurant, The Garden Hotel, Shanghai

Dale Keller, Bungalow Suite, Amanusa Resort Hotel, Bali

Tessa Kennedy, ISID, The Balmoral Suite, Claridge's, London

Rebecca Key, 'Sparks' Boutique, Baltimore

Nancy Kwok, MCSD, Citibank, Tai Po, Hong Kong

Ricardo Lazo, Tlaxcala Fabric Showroom, Mexico City

Cynthia Leftwich, ASID, IBD, Office Renovation, Texas

Makoto Maehara, Bank of Tokyo, Tokyo

Vinicio Montalvo, Dental Offices, Santiago

Seiichi Nakagawa, 'Erard' Restaurant, Tokyo

Joshua Jih Pan, AIA, Performing Arts Hall, Taipei

Carlos A. Profet, Meta Corporation, Aruba

German Quiroga, Convention Center, Acapulco

Gerd Ramstad, Medical Facility, Oslo

Petra Schleifenheimer, Corporate Lobby, Nuremberg

Der Scutt, FAIA, Trump Tower Atrium, New York City

Rohini Shanker, Larsen and Toubro Limited, Madras

Yozo Shibata, Lounge Bar, The Garden Hotel, Shanghai

Chatchawal Submuang, Convention Center Reception Hall, Bangkok

David I. Tay, Display, The Empress Palace, Singapore

Victor Tom, ASID, CSID, Executive Suite, Caesar Park Hotel, Taiwan

Jacob Tsang, Post-Modern Restaurant, Toronto

Gaby Widajanti, Executive Board Room, Jakarta

Evan Michael Williams, Grand Lido Hotel, Jamaica

Ayako Yahagi, Corporate Lobby, Tokyo

Jaci Yoap, Gallery Showroom, Wisconsin

Reflecting a new style in Japanese design, the Kaniya Restaurant in Tokyo features a courtyard-like atmosphere in bright primary colors. Interior design: Seiichi Nakagawa. Photography: Koshi Miwa.

Roberto Alcantara

*F*ounder of Spacio Planeacion y Diseño in Mexico City, Roberto Alcantara has developed a successful blend of design expertise and management efficiency during his career. Working as both architect and general manager, Mr. Alcantara has created a highly efficient design team of six architects, two graphic designers, an industrial designer, two illumination advisors and two civil engineers, plus a support staff. Backed by this qualified team, his firm has enjoyed tremendous growth and development since 1990, having successfully completed more than 120 commercial, residential, office and institutional projects throughout Mexico.

"*C*ontemporary styling combines with practicality in this executive office. To accent the room's distinctive emphasis on art, the design lines were kept simple while incorporating interesting modifications. The room's focal point centers on four paintings individually displayed in recessed alcoves on one of the walls adjacent to the windows. The paintings are paired vertically, with the left and right alcoves separated by a wide, slightly extruding panel. Lush flourishing plants complete the ambience of this office, providing its executive with comfort and convenience for critical business meetings or a few moments of personal reflection and repose before moving on to the next item on the agenda."

Roberto Alcantara, Spacio Planeacion y Diseno SA de CV
Lira #33, Col. Prados de Coyoacan, Mexico City CP 04810 DF, Mexico
Tel.: (52) 5-679-9813, Fax: (52) 5-679-9813

Photography: Bernardo Fuchs

160

Sinee Amoradhat

*A*rchitectural design was the profession Sinee Amoradhat pursued in her studies. She received her Bachelor of Architecture degree from Chulalongkorn University in 1977 and went on to finish her Master of Architecture studies at Carnegie-Mellon University in 1978. As a registered professional architect, Ms. Amoradhat is a member of the Association of Siamese Architects in her native Thailand. She began her career with Design 103 Limited in 1979, and earned the respect of her colleagues as she worked in several capacities before being named Director in 1992. Her major projects have ranged from residential and vacation homes to commercial and hotel designs. These include offices for Union Carbide Thailand Company, Ltd., offices for Malaysian Airlines, the head office of The Government Housing Bank in Bangkok, various facilities for Thai Shell Exploration and Production Company, Ltd., the extension of The Royal Netherlands Embassy in Bangkok, and the master plan for Bang Bua Thong Land Development, comprising a housing project and sports complex in Nonthaburi.

"*M*odern function merges with historical architecture in the design of the Queen Sirikit National Convention Center cafeteria in Bangkok. As throughout the entire convention center, the design theme was to represent Thai life, and the cultures of the four major regions of Thailand. This room is an example of the architecture of the central region during the late nineteenth century. Blended with the Thai-Western style through the use of wooden fretwork decor, the large vaulted ceiling of reflective glass and open metal framing creates a spacious, outdoor atmosphere for casual dining.

"*C*risp white patio-styled chairs are cushioned in a multi-colored print, lending a tropical feeling. The primary color is green, used both on the ceiling framework and the tabletops. Dark, broad-leafed plants and trees add further accent both in terms of color and tropical style. The natural wood tones of the fretwork are repeated throughout the space – in the decorative planters positioned around the room, in the traditionally styled gazebo, the railing separating the food service line from the dining area, and again in trim running the length of the room above the soffit.

"*T*he food service area is set back under a normal height ceiling and comprises a modern, efficient service bar, illuminated by recessed ceiling panels and spot lighting. Supporting columns are finished in an off-white, as are some of the walls. The flooring is sectioned by a grid pattern which echoes the framing overhead, also accented in shades of green – a customary color used in Thai decorating and architecture. It was in this tradition that the room was fashioned, establishing an informal tropical dining area true to the Thai-Western heritage of culture and design."

Sinee Amoradhat, Design 103 Limited
8th-9th, 14th Floors, Asoke Tower Office Building
219 Asoke Road, Sukhumvit 21, Bangkok 10110, Thailand
Tel.: (66) 2-260-0160-7, Fax: (66) 2-260-0230, 2-259-0489, 2-259-1191

Katherine (Bettle) Bacon

Katherine Bacon graduated in Interior Design with highest honors, and in 1985 became president of The Finishing Touch, Inc. She has appeared weekly on Canadian television as the interior design specialist for the *Noon Hour Show*. She is at this time furthering her studies in Architectural Technology at the Granton Institute in Toronto to complement her chosen profession. Katherine Bacon specializes in both commercial and residential projects and is a member of I.D.N.B. Her major projects include the York Point Condominiums, executive offices of Baxter Foods, Ltd., The Brenan Group of Funeral Homes, Fundy Cablevision Corporate Headquarters and the project shown here, The New Brunswick Telephone Company Corporate Center.

"*I* wanted to create a tranquil, efficient, yet visionary atmosphere for this high technology telecommunications facility. My theme was Planet Earth, the globe. I used a state-of-the-art carpet pattern as a major focal point, with colors selected to represent the planet as seen from outer space. This color scheme is unique to this corporate center, with black and grey to invoke a high tech image, plum to convey the warmth of the planet, and aqua to represent the oceans. I selected all natural substances of mahogany, granite, and leather to give a solid, prestigious feeling of strength and quality. For contrast, I used sophisticated elements in stainless steel and the highly functional lines of the furnishings to add a definite futuristic aspect. As a final dramatic stroke, the entire space is illuminated by strategically-placed high intensity quartz lighting."

Katherine Bacon, The Finishing Touch, Inc.
101-105 Charlotte Street, St. John, New Brunswick, Canada E2L 2J2
Tel.: (506) 633-1358, Fax: (506) 632-4064

Photography: Martin Flewwelling

162

Ernesto Francisco Bedmar

*T*he creative career of Ernesto Bedmar spans both architectural and interior design projects, and he utilizes his skills for both residential and commercial clients. Born in Cordoba, Argentina, Mr. Bedmar crossed the seas to establish a flourishing interior design firm in Singapore. Ernesto also finds time to tutor and instruct at the National University so other designers can benefit from his design experience.

*"W*hen approached to design the Kimin Collection, a specialized antique gallery, I realized the quality of the antiques would demand a unique setting. The rectangular space in Le Meridien Hotel is surrounded by clear glass walls, so people walking the adjacent corridors enjoy a glimpse of the interior. The gallery's formal sitting arrangement imitates home or office interiors to help clients visualize how the antiques will look in their own setting. Partitions are varied in height and their arrangements are staggered, each designed with windows and cut-in shelves so they can function as display cabinets as well. This combination of utility and artistic design allows clients to treasure both what they take home as well as the time spent at the gallery."

Ernesto Francisco Bedmar, Bedmar & Shi Designers Pte., Ltd.
11 Dhoby Ghaut #08-09, Cathay Building, Singapore 0922
Tel.: (65) 336-5022, Fax: (65) 339-0010

Photography: Seow Cheong Heng

165

Consuelo Boom

Born in Mexico City, Maria del Consuelo Boom earned her architectural degree from Intercontinental University in 1986. Her work has ranged from reconstruction projects after the Mexico City earthquake to designing furniture for a jewelry center to the renovation of an amusement park in Acapulco. Additional projects include an ecological house in Tlalpuente, an aerobics club in Mexico City, and residential designs throughout Mexico.

"**W**hen laying out the floorplan for this retail furniture showroom in Mexico City, I wanted to create as much 'transparency' as possible, so customers would have the sensation of being in an open area. Neutral colors are used for the carpet, walls and ceiling in order to let the furniture and decorating pieces stand out. The two exceptions are the raised wood plank walkway running the length of the ground level, and the turquoise pipe railing on the staircase and catwalk leading to the second level. Additional accents were created with trim colors, various finishes, wallpapers and moldings. Overhead tracks of spot lamps and dropped halogen lamps provide brilliant accent lighting to the displays and furniture, enticing customers to choose treasures for their own homes."

Maria del Consuelo Boom, Muebleria Frey, S.A. de C.V.
Perferico Sur 5128, Pedregal de Carrasco, Mexico City DF 04700, Mexico
Tel.: (52) 5-665-6566, Fax: (52) 5-666-1668

Photography: Ernesto J. Torres

Moon-Young Choi

*K*orean designer Moon-Young Choi specializes in commercial and residential interior architecture and design. He received his Bachelor of Fine Arts degree from Hong-Ik University in Seoul, and his Interior Design Diploma from England's Rhodec School. Mr. Choi has been the principal designer of Kofuco Interiors Co., Ltd. since 1988. His recent projects include the Paradise Hotel Sogwipo, Polo-Ralph Lauren stores, and several major branch offices for Citibank.

"*T*o introduce 'CitiGold', a new banking concept in Korea, Citibank, N.A. wanted an entirely different approach to their interior planning and design. This design had to incorporate Citibank's state-of-the-art banking systems in a small, 1200 square foot facility, while creating a private, exclusive feeling appropriate to the CitiGold concept. I began this design by selecting a mahogany panelling to create the feeling and intimacy of a residential library. As a contrast, I allowed subtle green tones to dominate the upholstered pieces, the wall covering and the patterned carpet. For illumination, I designed large circular ceiling recesses to diffuse the lighting and provide a soft play of illumination and shadow. For accent lighting I used small, shaded table-and wall-lamps. The furnishings include skirted, tailored chairs and sofas which reinforce the home-like atmosphere. A feeling of nature is also present, with sky blue above, mossy greens below and rich woods all around. Though a functioning office, this interior is anything but officious."

Moon-Young Choi, Kofuco Interiors Co., Ltd.
957 Konghang-Dong, Kangshu-Ku, Seoul, Korea
Tel.: (82) 2-665-1141, Fax: (82) 2-661-1141

Solichin Gunawan, HDII

Drawing from his expertise in the field of interior architecture, Solichin Gunawan has developed an innovative architectural and interior design firm in his native Indonesia. He was educated at Bandung Institute of Technology, and is a member of the Indonesian Society of Interior Designers. Mr. Gunawan's projects include hotels, restaurants, banks and convention centers in Indonesia, Japan, and the United States. His most notable work includes ARCO's Indonesian headquarters and the Grand Hotel Preanger. His favorite, however, is the project illustrated here, the Puri Agung Hall of the Sahid Jaya Hotel, which he completed with his partner, Mr. Abendanu Moeljono, and associate, Ms. Mawly Suraya.

"The design concept for Puri Agung, Sahid Jaya Hotel's main hall in Jakarta, was to recreate the grand tradition and splendor of an audience hall of the old Javanese Royal Palace, while keeping within the parameters of a modern, Western-oriented hotel. The tradition of Javanese design required supporting columns patterned from the center to the edges of the hall, with minimal wall structure. Modern function necessitated fully-enclosed, unobstructed floor space. Our design approach compromised with a radiating pattern in the ceiling from the center chandelier using open-beam framing. Traditional decoration, heavily based in Javanese mythology, enrich the walls and ceiling, all handcrafted and painted with Javanese techniques handed down over the centuries. Since the hall was to be used for events ranging from elaborate weddings and formal receptions to simple seminars, traditional colors, proportions and forms were adapted to meet the more contemporary needs and the ambience of modern hotel operation. In total, my intentions for a strong design statement and a sense of place were both met."

Solichin Gunawan, HDII, P.T. Atelier 6 Interior
Jalan Cikini IV / 20-A, Jakarta, Indonesia 10330
Tel.: (62) 21-310-0276, Fax: (62) 21-310-3396

Photography: Rudy Sugiharto (left); Hilman Maulani (above).

Masae Kawamura, JID, JIA

*M*ulti-faceted hotel interior design projects are standard for Masae Kawamura, Executive Director of Kanko Kikaku Sekkeisha, Yozo Shibata & Associates, the prestigious design firm based in Tokyo. Projects have taken him to Singapore, Sri Lanka, Turkey and the People's Republic of China. His myriad restaurant and hotel design projects illustrate the creativity and talent Mr. Kawamura brings to each assignment. Often encompassing a wide range of uses of space and facility needs, it is not uncommon that a single hotel project would include guest rooms, restaurants, lounges, meeting rooms, ballrooms, retail shops, pool areas, gymnasiums and other recreational facilities.

*M*r. Kawamura has been involved in the development and design of numerous hotel facilities, including the Hilton International Tokyo, ANA Hotel Tokyo, ANA Hotel Kanazawa in Japan, Garden Hotel Shanghai China, Sapporo Royal Hotel in Japan, Century Royal Sapporo in Japan, Swissôtel the Bosphorus Istanbul, and ANA Hotel Sydney (36th Floor). He is a member of the Japan Institute of Architects and the Japan Interior Designers Association.

"*E*legant formality was my goal for this restaurant in the Garden Hotel Shanghai. Throughout the entire design, I worked with the contrast of light and dark, both in terms of the lighting and the color scheme. I designed the illumination to effect a subdued yet dramatic mood. To accomplish this, I selected a unique mix of spot lighting fixtures, using different sizes, colors, and intensities of brightness to imbue fascinating patterns of shadow and reflection in a relaxed, intimate atmosphere.

"*B*rass was used as an integral design element. I used this metal to accentuate the lighting aura of the room, beginning with the perimeter of the large rectangular room, which was edged with brass-colored trim framing the top and bottom of the soffit. Brass was also used for the floor-to-ceiling trim defining the individual wall sections. Warm, reflective brass accents are repeated throughout the room in the track lighting and recessed spot fixtures. An especially effective application is the lighting fixture illuminating the gold-on-black mural centered on one wall.

"*S*traight-back dining chairs provide comfortable seating at tables designed in size to accommodate parties of two to ten. Brass and gold continue to accent the decor, this time in the table settings. Platters for large parties, cutlery, and selected dinnerware pieces all reflect the grandeur of the room. Rich burgundy, beige and creams are the dominant colors I chose, contrasting the light table linens and napkins with the darker carpet and chair fabrics. With each detail in place, all contrasts blend into a harmonious elegance that makes dining in this restaurant a truly memorable experience during one's stay in Shanghai."

Masae Kawamura, JID, JIA, Kanko Kikaku Sekkeisha, Yozo Shibata & Associates
No. 9 Mori-Building, 1-2-3 Atago, Minato-Ku, Tokyo, 105 Japan
Tel.: (81) 3-3434-4674, Fax: (81) 3-3434-5406, 3-3434-2297

Dale Keller

After receiving his B.A. from the University of Washington, Dale Keller did graduate study at the University of Tokyo's School of Architecture. In 1955, he founded Dale Keller & Associates. DKA has designed the interiors of over one hundred international hotels, palaces, office buildings and private residences, including the Okura Hotel in Tokyo, The Regent Hotel in Hong Kong, and Beijing Lufthansa Centre (Kempinski) in Beijing.

"In the design of this bungalow suite for the Amanusa Resorts Hotel in southern Bali, our goal was to maintain harmony and compatibility between the design, its setting and the cultural environment. The bed and living area is dominated by a queensize four-poster bed, draped and canopied in gauzy white. Its railing and headboard echo the high drama created by the dark, rich textures of the ceiling. The bath and dressing area features twin vanities, shower, toilet and luggage space. The sunken bath appears to float in a reflection pool contained within a private courtyard. The overall result is a suite with a distinctive elegance of a colonial home in the tropics."

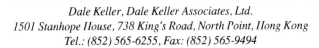

Dale Keller, Dale Keller Associates, Ltd.
1501 Stanhope House, 738 King's Road, North Point, Hong Kong
Tel.: (852) 565-6255, Fax: (852) 565-9494

Photography: Jeff Kilpatrick

174

Tessa Kennedy, ISID

*F*irmly established in London as one of Europe's leading interior designers, Tessa Kennedy has developed her distinguished reputation over 25 years as a designer. Her clients include H.M. the King of Jordan, Candice Bergen, Rudolf Nureyev and George Harrison. Ms. Kennedy is President of the British Chapter of the International Society of Interior Designers and was recently voted International Vice President of Membership. Her projects have appeared in *House & Garden, Architectural Digest,* and *Vogue.*

"*H*otel accommodations must be memorable, and fortunately Claridge's in London agreed, giving me the opportunity to recreate the romance of Scotland's Highlands for this hotel suite. I painted the walls in *faux bois* to create a paneled room to match the pine fireplace, and then filled the room with tartans in the same colors and scale. The sofa is covered in a leaf green velvet which I found in America. Photographs of my children in kilts and tartan suits adorn the tables, while the tapestries depict Gothic castles, lochs and glens. It was exciting to see how such an anonymous room becomes warm and inviting, creating a delightful atmosphere for every hotel guest fortunate enough to experience this fabulous suite."

Tessa Kennedy, ISID, Tessa Kennedy Design Ltd.
Studio 5, 91/97 Freston Road, London W11 4BD, England
Tel.: (44) 71-221-4546, Fax: (44) 7-229-2899, L.A. Fax: (310) 273-9948

Photography: Simon Brown (room), James Mortimer for World of Interiors (portrait).

Rebecca Key

Commercial interior designer Rebecca Key was born in Baltimore, and received her Bachelor of Architecture degree from the University of Maryland in 1977. She later attended the Maryland Institute of Art. Formerly the director of store planning at Webster Clothes, Inc., Ms. Key has been president of Alexander Key and Associates since 1983. Her major projects include the U.S. Naval Academy Uniform Store, University of Maryland Medical Systems Gift Shop and Pharmacy, and the Charlestown Retirement Community.

"As a new accessory store, 'Sparks' needed to be colorful and contemporary in its design. My client wanted a look that dramatically reflected the store's name. I began with a flooring design of inter-connecting circles of porcelain ceramic tile within a setting of darker carpeting. These shapes are reflected overhead in the ceiling design of concentric circles positioned at varying depths. I then had the edges of the ceiling circles painted in alternating shades of vivid aqua and magenta, ringed with thin bands of neon to highlight their brightness. For contrast, the lowest interiors were left in a more restful tone, and the gridded acoustical tile hanging above the carpeted areas is neutral colored. The circle patterns of both the floor and the ceiling were extended to the shop's exterior, giving the entrances a 'welcome mat' below, and a canopy for the neon sign above. The blue and magenta tones were repeated in the walls, which were then sponge- and rag-painted. These colors demand notice, and bring attention to the store's colorful wares. The circular motif is continued in the curved design of the counters and on through to the half-column legs of the display stands."

Rebecca Key, Alexander Key and Associates
2129 Maryland Avenue, Baltimore, Maryland 21218
Tel.: (410) 962-5365, Fax: (410) 962-7324

Photography: Linda Johnson

Nancy Kwok, MCSD

Since the start of her career in 1972, Nancy Kwok has developed exceptional expertise in all areas of interior design. Her projects include commercial and residential designs, as well as hotels and restaurants. Her formal education was obtained at the Hong Kong Polytechnic and L'Alliance Française de Hong Kong. Ms. Kwok worked for several prominent design firms before bringing her skills and talents to set up her own design practice, Hinex Universal Design Contracting Co. Ltd., in 1986, where she serves as Chief Designer and Managing Director. Among her numerous projects are interior designs for the Bank of China Shenzhen Headquarters in China, the headquarters for the Xin Hua News Agency in Macau, the Gloria Plaza Hotel in Beijing, and S.Z. Development Center Hotel in China.

"Function, accessibility, and a professional, yet comfortable, atmosphere for both the client and their customers were a few of the factors I needed to address during this project. This Citibank office in Tai Po, Hong Kong, has a high traffic volume, so I chose straight, clean lines for the reception and customer service area, keeping the space as barrier-free as possible. Dropped-ceiling panels serve to define work areas, thereby eliminating the need for excessive partitions or restrictive, permanent architectural elements. Recessed lighting was designed with the specific use of each area in mind. This approach allows functional lighting for the computer and work stations, and a more decorative illumination for the main reception counter, where lights were mounted under the extended counter, bathing it in a soft glow. The track lighting was positioned to dramatically spotlight the corporation's logo on the wall behind the main counter.

"In keeping with the traditional culture of Hong Kong, red was chosen as the room's predominant color. I covered the entire wall behind the main reception counter in red, using a bright white for the raised, three-dimensional logo. The chairs and the inlaid carpet sections defining the chair space are in the same vibrant shade. While red is used even on the advertising pieces, I selected neutral colors for the one-piece counters and work surfaces for contrast. These muted tones also serve to blend the furnishing with the computer equipment, thereby reinforcing the uniformity of the area and creating a clean, uncluttered look even though the components are of varied sizes and shapes.

"Furnishings were kept simple to maintain the sleek design of the room, particularly at the work stations where customers would interact with the staff. Throughout the area, fabrics and finishes were chosen for both durability and pleasing appearance. Every detail was carefully considered, and the result is a professional, relaxed atmosphere, and a perfect invitation to the bank's customers."

Nancy Kwok, MCSD, Hinex Universal Design Contracting Co., Ltd.
4501, China Resources Building, 26, Harbour Road, Wanchai, Hong Kong
Tel.: (852) 827-8077, Fax: (852) 827-7919

Ricardo Lazo

Originally involved in architecture, Ricardo Lazo's interests and talents broadened first into interior design and then into textile design, which has become his specialization. Born in Mexico, Ricardo decided to create his own fabric designs to give a distinctive accent to his interior design projects. He chose to maintain a cultural authenticity to his fabrics, giving them the same textures as those created on traditional hand looms. In 1979, he introduced his concepts to the market, and refurbished an abandoned 19th century fabric factory in Tlaxcala to use as his manufacturing center. His fabrics were an immediate success with interior designers throughout the world.

"Cultural heritage in design is important to me, and the reception space of the Tlaxcala office strongly reflects this philosophy. Following this concept, the sitting area is centered around a sofa covered in materials of my own design. Accenting this, the table, chairs and other pieces are all of the same mahogany wood. The floor is paved with hand-made reproduction *barro Mexicano* tiles, covered with a traditional area rug. Art pieces include an 18th century painting by the Mexican artist Miguel Cabrera, as well as 19th century Talavera ceramic pieces. Accenting these traditional furnishings are samples of my fabric collection, on display for clients to examine. These fabric designs are the result of merging traditional pre-Colombian and more modern Novohispanic cultures, thereby creating a unique contemporary Mexican style."

Ricardo Lazo, Richardo Lazo Textiles
Insurgentes Sur 2047-C, San Angel DF CP 01000, Mexico
Tel.: (52) 5-661-1197, (52) 5-661-9196, Fax: (52) 5-661-9196

Photography: Daniel Nierman

Cynthia Leftwich, ASID, IBD

*A*s a commercial interior designer, Cynthia Leftwich has worked on a variety of contract projects including banks, hospitals, medical office suites and restaurants. She attended both the University of Texas at Arlington and Texas Tech University. Ms. Leftwich received the Achievement Award for Restoration in 1986, and has been listed in numerous editions of Barons *Who's Who in Interior Design.*

"*P*reservation of the past and anticipation of the future were the two concepts I needed to blend in this adapted reuse of a downtown warehouse. This space was converted into business offices on the first level and a design and art studio on the lower level. I wanted to preserve the structural ambience of lofty, open space so the ceiling structure, HVAC system and original pendant lighting were refurbished and left in place. The original brick walls were sanded and sealed, then the office space was defined with eight-foot partitions of drywall that were painted and finished with wooden crown molded base and framing. The original hardwood flooring was refinished and then accentuated with a custom designed rug to complement geometric shapes and forms repeated throughout the space. Black, natural wood and brick colors were used as a subtle accent to the visual and architectural features of the original building."

Cynthia Leftwich, ASID, IBD, Leftwich & Associates
1711 Avenue J, Suite 108, Lubbock, Texas 79401
Tel.: (806) 747-5584, Fax: (806) 762-2044

Photography: Robert Suddarth

184

Makoto Maehara, JID

With expertise in many areas of design, Makoto Maehara works as a commercial and residential interior designer, as well as a furniture designer. He completed his education at the Tokyo National University of Fine Arts and Music. Mr. Maehara is currently an interior planner and designer at the Maehara Makoto Design Room in Tokyo. His major projects include the interior and exterior design of numerous banks, hotels, restaurants, offices, and homes throughout Asia.

"I wanted to create a feeling of trust, warmth and personal service in this design for the Bank of Tokyo. I began by designing this branch without the typical counters which separate tellers from patrons — business here is conducted at desks in small, private spaces. These spaces are separated by special partitions, made of a liquid crystal composite glass which electronically changes from clear to opaque at the touch of a button. The carpeting, lighting, wall and ceiling finishes, and accessory items were all selected to bring a relaxed, almost residential feeling into a business setting. With its warm colors and subdued dignity, this bank interior promotes the sense of trust and security I was striving for."

Makoto Maehara, Maehara Makoto Design Room
1-25-5 Yutenji, Meguro-ku, Tokyo 153, Japan
Tel.: (81) 3-3710-0736, Fax: (81) 3-3710-0736

Photography: Yuzuru Shimizu

Vinicio Montalvo

*A*s president of A.C.M. & M Arquitectos Asociados in Santiago, Chile, Vinicio Montalvo oversees design assignments for hotels, restaurants, factories, malls, residential buildings and clinics. Together with associates Alvaro Matus Correa and Ricardo Cabrera Grossy, his firm has completed over 900,000 square feet of architectural and interior designs in Chile, Argentina and Ecuador.

"*T*echnology and aesthetics were the two elements my associates and I needed to bring together in the design of this modern dental clinic in Santiago. Designed to care for eight adults and eight children simultaneously, efficient use of space and materials was mandatory, but we did not want to create a sterile environment in the process. The main reception area was kept spacious and barrier-free to comfortably accommodate a high volume of patient and staff movement. Atrium-style window panels provide natural lighting to brighten the area. We selected a mix of traditional and contemporary leather furniture for comfortable, relaxed seating. Antique art pieces and unusual sculptures were used as focal points around the room, with wall-sized paintings and hand-painted murals as a final treatment of the walls. The result is a professional yet friendly environment that is also extremely functional with all the technological conveniences of a modern healthcare facility."

Vinicio Montalvo, A.C.M. & M Arquitectos Asociados
Callo 3227, Las Condes, Santiago, Chile
Tel.: (56) 2-233-3088, Fax: (56) 2-233-1989

Photography: Luis Hernan Herros Infante

Seiichi Nakagawa, JID

Seiichi Nakagawa, a Certified Interior Planner, took his degree in Industrial Design at Musashino Fine Arts College. He's currently a designer and executive with the Interior Design Department of MHS Planners, Architects & Engineers. He received the Design Achievement Award at the Commercial Environment Design Exhibit in 1986. Seiichi Nakagawa's major projects include the Daiichi Hotel Tokyo Seafort, the Musahi-Fuji Country Club, the ANA Computer Center, the corporate office of Nikka Whiskey, and this Restaurant "Erard" of Tsumura, Inc.

"My design image for this seafood restaurant was the 1920's Cotton Club with its Dixieland jazz and Art Deco style. To recreate the look of this American period style in Tokyo, I used period elements to create a historical evidence of the era, and exaggerated the pieces that would be most recognizable by the restaurant's Japanese clientele. Of course, I wanted visiting Americans to have a sense of recognition too. I wanted to evoke a feeling of being underground, in a typical 1920's American speakeasy. I began this design with the bare wood floors, and then used high intensity ceiling lighting for the illumination. The space is furnished with large dark granite tables and upholstered straight-back chairs. The Art Deco theme was completed with the accessory pieces, using period lamps, sculptures, and framed prints."

Seiichi Nakagawa, JID, MHS Planners, Architects & Engineers
1-5-17, Moto Akasaka, Minato-ku, Tokyo, Japan 107
Tel.: (81) 3-3403-6161, Fax: (81) 3-3404-6515

Photography: Toshiharu Kitajima

190

Joshua Jih Pan, AIA

Registered as a professional architect in New York, New Jersey and the Republic of China, Joshua Jih Pan received bachelors degrees in Architecture from Rice University and the National Taiwan Cheng Kung University. He received his Master of Science degree in Architecture and Urban Design from Columbia University. After extensive work in the United States, Mr. Pan established J.J. Pan and Partners in Taipei in 1981. He has won major design awards throughout Taiwan.

"Welcome to the Performing Hall of the National Chiao Tung University in Taiwan. Although this theatre seats 350 people, I wanted to create a feeling of intimacy as well as drama. Since limited land was available for wing stages, I designed extensive 'backstage' support space beneath the stage. To accommodate the multi-functional demands of the hall, a state-of-the-art theater lighting and audio control system was incorporated into the interior design. To add warmth, I carpeted the space in a soft pastel, accented with natural stained wood railings. The installation of indirect illumination completed this design, with light shining from the zig-zag acoustical side walls and giving a spirited mood to the entire hall."

Joshua Jih Pan, AIA, J.J. Pan & Partners
21, Alley 12, Lane 118, Ren Ai Road, Sec. 3, Taipei, Taiwan
Tel.: (886) 2-701-2617, Fax: (886) 2-700-4489

Carlos Profet

*A*ruban interior designer Carlos A. Profet, born in 1955, received a Dutch education in Aruba and Holland. Mr. Profet studied interior design at the CE-Art Academy in Bogota, receiving a B.F.A. Degree. After a year of free-lancing in Aruba and Curacao, he studied environmental design at Parson's School of Design in New York City, receiving another B.F.A. Degree in 1982. Since 1983, Mr. Profet has been Owner/Director of Inarch N.V.

"*T*his project, the corporate offices for Meta Corporation, is located on the first floor of an existing steel-frame building with almost no view or natural light. My challenge here was to compensate for these shortcomings from within the space by means of color and transparency. Glass blocks positioned as interior windows create the illusion of greater visual access to the outdoors. Large, clear panes are positioned diagonally among smaller, frosted ones for variety and interest. The diagonal axis of this 6,500 square-foot area has been strongly stressed to break away from its basically box-like proportions as evidenced by the L-shaped free-standing wall, at right, and the series of recessed walls set perpendicular to it. Curved elements such as the large dark column and fluted counter further serve to relieve the space's squareness, while white walls and ceilings open up and lighten the natural darkness. The total design scheme creates a modern and fashionable work environment in which the many varied departments of the corporation can operate as an efficient unified entity. "

Carlos A. Profet, Inarch
Vondellaan 19 B, Oranjestad, Aruba
Tel.: (297) 8-25677, Fax: (297) 8-32574

Photography: Fernando Rafael Luidens

German Quiroga

*A*rchitectural designer German Quiroga completed his studies in industrial design, and went on to develop numerous projects in this field. For the past twenty-three years, he has been a leading international designer of custom office furniture, all manufactured in his own factory. Multi-talented, Mr. Quiroga also specializes in the development and design of public gathering places such as convention centers, theaters and exposition halls.

"*T*he *Salas del Parque Papagayo* in Acapulco posed the challenge of designing a space that will equally fit the needs of various functions. This space needed to serve as a theater, a convention hall, and exposition center as well as a conference and assembly room. Of prime importance in the design of such a vast space is the fusion of architectural and decor elements. With this in mind, I used very few materials and almost no color. I treated the walls as individual entities, avoiding the monotony of perpendicular planes. The large central floor space is ceramic tile while the less-traveled perimeter areas around the pyramids and buttressed walls are covered with darker carpeting. The natural striations of the pyramids' concrete surfaces give them an organic appearance and their black bases make them appear to hover above the floor. Mirrors function as moldings at many of the wall-ceiling joints, reflecting form and light. I used the large concrete cross-beams to lower the central ceiling level and augment the light provided by the smaller recessed fixtures. The prevailing grayness of the room allows the public to provide the real color."

German Quiroga, Intermobel Office Furniture, SA de CV
Ave. Torres de Ixtapantongo #380, Col. Olivar los Padres, Mexico DF, 01780
Tel.: (52) 5-595-8667, Fax: (52) 5-595-1589

Photography: Sigbjorn Lenes

Gerd Ramstad

*I*n her native Norway, Gerd Ramstad is a commercial and residential interior designer and architect. A graduate of Bergen University, Ms. Ramstad has won numerous international awards for contract interior design, as well as finalist awards for her furniture designs. Her work has been exhibited in Helsinki's Habitare and the Museum of Modern Art in Kyoto, Japan. Based in Jar, near Oslo, Ms. Ramstad focuses on shops, schools, hotels and hospitals. Her major projects include interior design work for the University Kristiansand, the Klekken Hotel, and the main offices of Norway's Nordberg Group. The project shown here was nominated for the Designer's Establishment of the Year.

"*T*his salon for the Montebello Recreation Center was designed with the intention of providing a cheerful environment for the recuperation of post-hospital cancer patients. I selected rose tones as the primary coloration for their soothing yet uplifting qualities. The shades run from nearly pink on the walls, to true rose in the delicately patterned draperies, to nearly burgundy as seen in the upholstery of the game area chairs. I had stripes painted along the wall summits to reflect the medium and dark tones and to accentuate the warmth of the moldings. This treatment also creates the illusion of lower ceilings, giving the room a more intimate feeling. The tables, bookshelves and custom chess set are all of my own design, for which I selected woods with a glow of rosy warmth, adding to the residential atmosphere of the room.

"*F*or the accent color, I selected the serene yet vibrant contrast of teal blue. This cooler hue is used in the chair fabric and area rugs to define conversation areas. The furniture, though decidedly modern, have soft lines and are warm, comfortable and inviting. The two large, gray 'ball' chairs in the rear of the room not only provide seating but also function as pieces of sculptural art.

"*A*lthough natural wood predominates, a quartet of chairs is painted black to add depth and to accent the grand piano. Traditional lighting fixtures, a few plants and a profusion of books combine with the soft window treatments to complement the contemporary furnishings. Despite the fact that this is a public room, the general atmosphere is that of a comforting contemporary home."

Gerd Ramstad, Gerd Ramstad Interiorarkitekt Nil
Lovenskioldsvei 16-B, 1342 Jar, Norway
Tel.: (47) 2-53-04-58, Fax: (47) 2-12-34-10

Petra Schleifenheimer

*B*orn in Bavaria, Petra Schleifenheimer was educated at the Nuremberg Academy of Fine Arts, where she received her degree as an interior architect Diplom-Ingeníeur in 1981. In 1985, after three years as a design interior architect with Firma Reim, she launched her career as an independent interior designer in western Germany. Since that time she has also been a consultant for Schickedanz Warehouse Company. In addition to many private residences, Petra Schleifenheimer's projects include the Lollipop retail clothing store, the offices of KVDB-Automobile Club, LGB-Toy Factory, Kahle Copyshops, and the showroom, casino, offices, and film room of the BIG Toy Factory. Her projects have been published in numerous German magazines.

"*T*he entrance lobby of the BIG Toy Factory in Nuremberg was part of a 10,000 square foot office design which challenged my skills as both an interior designer and interior architect. I wanted to create a strong ambience, using materials to embody the company's motto, 'solid as a buffalo.' I selected a white, Italian marble from Michelangelo's quarries for the walls, which form a backdrop for the framed artwork and offer a refreshing contrast with the deep glimmer of the dark Labrador floor. These dark floors, in turn, reflect the starlight effect of the lighting above. I kept the space open with the use of floor-to-ceiling glass panels, which can be turned into frosted glass at the touch of a button during private conferences. The glass panel hardware and mounting supports are painted the powerful shade of red associated with the company's trademark. Finally, for a main focal point, I selected a sculpture consisting of a large, heavy white marble ball which seems to glide effortlessly on a thin film of water atop the black pedestal base."

Petra Schleifenheimer, Innenarchitektin
Fuerther Strasse 91a, 8500 Nuremberg 80, Germany
Tel.: (49) 911-289042, Fax: (49) 911-284641

Photography: Sabine Ketzler

200

Der Scutt, FAIA

Der Scutt began his studies at Pennsylvania State University and received his Masters in Architecture at Yale. After serving as design partner with Swanke Hayden Connell & Partners, he founded his own firm, Der Scutt Architect, in 1981. Author of numerous architectural articles for professional journals, Mr. Scutt has been an architectural critic at Harvard, Pratt, Washington University and Yale, and has made frequent appearances on television and radio. His many awards include the American Institute of Architects, Distinguished Service Award, IES, 1976, and the Tucker Award of Design Excellence, Building Stone Institute, 1990. He is also a Fellow of the IES. He's held a variety of offices in major professional associations, including the Architectural League of New York, the New York Building Congress, and the U.S. Institute of Theatre Technology. Mr. Scutt's major projects can be seen throughout the Northeast U.S., especially New York City, including the U.S. headquarters of Hong Kong Bank, the Grand Hyatt Hotel, 100 UN Plaza Tower, The Corinthian, The Milan, and the design shown here, Trump Tower Atrium.

"**D**esigning Trump Tower was an exciting opportunity to work with an imaginative and creative client. The actual footprint is relatively small, but allowed for much vertical drama which I intensified by building in reflective surfaces. We chose materials and colors which would make people feel both exhilarated and entertained, feelings that should always be part of the shopping experience. Paul Goldberger, the New York Times critic, said, 'The atrium of Trump Tower may well be the most pleasant interior public space to be completed in New York in some time'."

Der Scutt, FAIA, Der Scutt Architect
44 West 28th Street, New York, New York 10001
Tel.: (212) 725-2300, Fax: (212) 481-7094

Photography: Norman McGrath

Rohini Shanker

*E*ast Indian designer Rohini Shanker graduated from the University of Wisconsin and has been in the design field in India and abroad for twenty-two years. Specializing in office design, Ms. Shanker works for a number of Indian, Japanese and other international corporations. A documentary on her work was shown at the Festival of India in New York as well as on the PBS program *India Speaks*.

"*T*he design for Larsen and Toubro Ltd., a Danish engineering corporation in Madras, was a challenging project. This executive lounge represents the quintessence of that challenge in which an invigorating atmosphere unites with a corporate identity of contemporary elegance. Walls of melamine, teak wood, brick and tinted glass separate the space from support staff areas on one side and executive offices on the other. I selected a gridded design concept in keeping with the grid on the reinforced concrete for the floors and precast concrete 'waffles' for the ceiling. The lighting by Philips is housed within the waffles. Stainless steel chairs from Classic Designs are upholstered in grained silver-gray leather, while small gray area rugs anchor the seating areas. Tables are of stainless steel, tinted glass and cork. Two works of contemporary Indian art enhance the atmosphere: a bronze and silver statue on a marble pedestal by Gopal and a circular wall hanging with silver tantric figures mounted on canvas by Yadav. However, the main graphic attraction here is the Mondrian-like use of grids throughout the space."

Rohini Shanker, Consultant on Interior Design
#15, 2nd Avenue, Harrington Road, Madras, India 600-031
Tel.: (91) 44-860-970, Fax: (91) 44-860-970

Photography: S. Asad

Yozo Shibata, JIA

*A*s President of Kanko Kikaku Sekkeisha, Yozo Shibata & Associates, Yozo Shibata has completed hundreds of major hotel and restaurant installations throughout Asia. During his thirty-year career in architectural and interior design, he has worked on projects in Japan, Singapore, Malaysia, Thailand, China, Sri Lanka and Turkey. Mr. Shibata's skill and mastery in hotel architecture and design is highly regarded by the Japan Hotel Equipment Association, of which he is vice chairman. In addition, he serves as director of the Japan Transport Consultants Association. Mr. Shibata holds memberships in the Japan Institute of Architects, the Architectural Institute of Japan, the Tokyo Society of Architects and Building Engineers, and the Tokyo Professional Architects Association. His major hotel projects include the Four Seasons Hotel 'Chinzanso' in Tokyo, Swissotel's 'The Bosphoru' in Istanbul, the Beijing Shangri-La Hotel, the Hilton International Colombo in Sri Lanka and the Bangkok Shangri-La Hotel in Thailand.

"*I*ntimacy and comfort were the themes I chose for this modern lounge bar in the Garden Hotel Shanghai. Although the function of the room is to accommodate a large number of hotel guests, it was necessary to create the illusion of small conversation areas so guests could relax by themselves or entertain business clients or friends. To achieve this ambience, I grouped four chairs around a small table to form each conversation area, then positioned these groupings around the perimeter of the room. The center of the room was left essentially barrier-free to facilitate traffic by guests and staff and to provide a sense of separateness between the groups. Architecturally, I offset sections of the wall on one side of the room to further enhance the atmosphere of intimacy.

"*F*urnishings in the room are sophisticated, contemporary, and comfortable. A grand piano is centered in the lounge adjacent to a recessed section of wall. The room's major focal point, however, is a large, modern pedestal which supports a towering floral arrangement. The small chrome-like tiles of the pedestal contrast pleasingly with the oversized ebony urn, drawing one's eye immediately upon entering the room. The bar is recessed into one of the walls with a tasteful, open display of glassware behind the counter, giving one the feeling it is more a part of the decor than the functioning unit that it is.

"*C*olors were kept soft and neutral for quiet formality, and are repeated in the carpet, upholstery and walls. In the same manner, patterns and materials were chosen for their ability to blend easily with the overall design scheme. Tabletops are black and white marble, with brass-colored metal pedestals. For further continuity, I selected dark woods throughout the lounge for the chairs, bar and coping, resulting in a sophisticated, subtle atmosphere that would be an inviting retreat any time during one's stay at the hotel."

Yozo Shibata, JIA, Kanko Kikaku Sekkeisha, Yozo Shibata & Associates
No. 9 Mori-Building, 1-2-3 Atago, Minato-Ku, Tokyo, 105 Japan
Tel.: (81) 3-3434-4674, Fax: (81) 3-3434-5406, 3-3434-2297

Photography: Thakerng Pringpuangkeo

Chatchawal Submuang

Multi-talented and creative, the skills of Chatchawal Submuang are highly evident in the numerous commercial and hospitality industry design projects he has created. Born in Thailand, Mr. Submuang was educated at the Silpakorn University in Bangkok, where he received a Bachelor of Fine Arts degree through the University's Faculty of Decorative Arts. After graduating, he began his career as an interior designer, increasing his professional skills as his assignments ranged from the Samitivej Hospital in Bangkok to the renovation of Hilton International Hotels in Singapore, Kuala Lumpur and Jakarta. Advancement to senior interior designer came with his move to Design 103 Limited in 1984, and just a year later he was promoted to Project Manager.

Mr. Submuang has had the opportunity to work on some unique design projects, two of which are the renovation of the Sala Chalermkrung Theater in Bangkok, and the standard furniture design for service stations of Esso Standard Thailand Ltd. His hotel and nightclub design projects include the 'Gold Mine' discotheque at the Hyatt Terraces Hotel in the Philippines, the 'Music Room' in the Jakarta Hilton, 'The Trap' member club located at the Singapore Shopping Center, and the 'Xanadu' discotheque in the Chosun Westin Hotel in Seoul. His commercial clients include the Thai Granite Company, Ltd., the Aquastar Company, Ltd., the Siam Cement Company, Ltd., and Philips Electrical Company of Thailand, Ltd.

"**C**ultural heritage and art are prominent elements reflected in the design of the reception hall of Bangkok's Queen Sirikit National Convention Center. The interior design was aimed at reflecting the art and culture of the central region of Thailand, while complementing the exterior architecture and design of the building itself. A prominent feature of the hall is the decorative wall behind the reception counter, which is covered with Thai silk and accentuated with brass trim in the 'Sinato' design – an ancient Thai art form. On the back panel is a miniature wall painting which depicts a traditional procession symbolizing a gathering of people – which, of course, is the purpose of this room.

"**S**urmounted by four elephant heads, 'Gaja Stampa' is the free-standing column supporting a cosmic sphere. Towering above all other features of the room, it draws the eye upward to the immense, open-framed ceiling which dramatically emphasizes the spaciousness of the hall. Red and green – the colors employed most frequently in ancient Thai architecture – were chosen as the room's primary colors. Bold, bright carpet tiles were arranged in a pattern adapted from a Thai form for a sense of modernity and for harmony with the framing in the ceiling. With all elements of the room in place, this reception hall at once exhibits Thai art and culture, while offering a warm welcome to everyone who enters."

Chatchawal Submuang, Design 103 Limited
8th-9th, 14th Floors, Asoke Tower Office Building
219 Asoke Road (Sukhumvit 21), Bangkok 10110, Thailand
Tel.: (66) 2-260-0160-7, Fax: (66) 2-260-0230, 2-259-0489, 2-259-1191

David I. Tay

Well known for his creativity and genius, David I. Tay, founder of David Tay and Associates Pte. Ltd., is highly regarded for his ability to handle projects of an extremely demanding nature. In Asia, Mr. Tay's clients include Citibank NA, The Mandarin Singapore, The Oberoi Group, United Overseas Bank, Hilton, and numerous other prestigious concerns. One of his favorite works is found in an old historical building in Singapore at The Empress Palace.

"Within this elegant hall lie many priceless works from the Han Dynasty of China. The hall expresses the magnificence of the culture and heritage of the Chinese civilization presented within an ambience of modern technology and design philosophy. A subtle play of light on smooth, cascading silk accents the background shadow scene where two concubines perform – to specially composed music – the ancient hair combing ritual. Here we try to re-enact the provocative and sensuous atmosphere as would be appreciated by the Emperor from his chamber. Below stands Han city revived from its mysterious past, evoked by silk scrolls of light, a tranquil moon within an elegant bamboo composition."

David I. Tay, David Tay & Associates
10 Anson Road, #30-16 International Plaza, Singapore 0207
Tel.: (65) 221-2716, Fax: (65) 224-8805

Victor A. Tom, ASID, CSID

A graduate of UCLA, Victor A. Tom founded Design Group A in Taipei in 1972. A one-time professor of design at Chung Yuan Christian University, Mr. Tom has long been a contributing editor to such publications as *Modern Home*, *Home Decoration* and *Taipei Housing Monthly*. Among his major projects are numerous commercial, hotel, restaurant and office interiors throughout the world.

"*T*his Executive Suite living room for the Caesar Park Hotel in southern Taiwan posed the challenge of a design that was stately in demeanor while suggesting the atmosphere of a south sea tropical island. To achieve this, I used color sparingly, but richly in the rosewood parquet floor, the luxurious silk Persian carpet and the oversized oil painting of tropical flowers. Textures play freely in the slate accent walls, the coffered ceiling with rattan inlay and bamboo trim, the sand colored upholstery of homespun slub cotton, and the rattan accent chairs and end tables. A lush tropical atmosphere is suggested by the sheer curtains which look on to an ocean view, the louvered doors into the bedroom, and the liberal use of large-leaf tropical plants throughout the suite."

Victor A. Tom, ASID, CSID, Design Group A
288 Kuang Fu South Road, 4th Floor, Suite 5, Taipei, Taiwan, ROC
Tel.: (886) 2-776-5506, Fax: (886) 2-731-5620

Jacob Tsang

Specializing in restaurant, retail and office design, Jacob Tsang is a graduate of the International Academy of Merchandising and Design, and the Ontario College of Art. As the principal interior designer for Toronto's Suika Design, Inc., Mr. Tsang has worked on projects throughout Canada.

"**D**esigned with faithfulness to tradition, I selected classical elements of Japanese detail and combined them with post-modern architecture and design for this restaurant in downtown Toronto. I maintained a very traditional Japanese monochromatic color scheme which focuses on black with light wood and yellow tones as primary contrasts. The main dining room is typical of the entire restaurant, which includes a party/meeting room, revolving sushi bar and a *kareoke* area, encompassing a total of thirty-five-hundred square feet. Seating at the bar is accommodated by black chairs. Wood trim blends naturally with the gold-tone metal trim of the glass food case and the supports for the display shelving.

"**G**roup seating throughout the rest of the main dining room was created with the illusion of traditional Japanese seating. Cciling-high frame work surrounds each booth and table, with louvered woodworking separating guests from adjacent tables. The effect simulates lower-than-normal seating. All woodwork is jet black, as is the fabric covering the seat backs. Tables are white with wood tone edging, completing the continuity of decor throughout the room. With such attention to detail, each patron can experience not only the fine Japanese cuisine, but the richness of Japanese tradition as they dine in this unique Toronto restaurant."

Jacob Tsang, Suika Design, Inc.
50 Weybright Court, Unit 13, Scarborough, Ontario, M1S 5A8, Canada
Tel.: (416) 609-3668, 258-6708, Fax: (416) 609-9998

Photography: Daisy Mo

Photography: Iwan Sarif

Gaby Widajanti, IAI

*I*nternational exposure to the profession of interior design came early to Gaby Widajanti as she pursued her education. After studying Architecture at Tarumanegara University, she traveled to Berlin's Technishe University where she graduated with honors in 1977. Ms. Widajanti gained experience in a variety of areas in her first position with Bent Severin, Singapore, where she was given responsibility for design coordination, office management, and marketing and presentation. In 1985, she started her own interior design firm in Jakarta, Ahara Prima Design, PT.

"*S*olid, simple design was my choice for this 1,300 square-foot boardroom for the Pt. Asuransi Insindo Taisho Insurance Company in Jakarta. The impressive natural wood table top is supported by two massive pedestals at either end of the table, which was designed to seat 18. The rectangular configuration, when fully utilized, sits six on each long side and three at both the head and foot of the table. The purpose of this room is to accommodate large groups of business executives and their entourage of portfolios, briefcases, and other accoutrements. With this in mind, I chose clean, simple design lines which included subtle ornamentation through the materials used in the furnishings themselves.

"*C*ropped corners actually give the table eight 'sides' instead of four, keeping end areas comfortably uncrowded, and providing the versatility to add four chairs if necessary. This shape is repeated on the surface of the table by inlaid strips of darker wood, and again by the light fixture centered over the length of the table. The opaque material of this light fixture is contrasted against its dark frame, and the contrast is echoed again in the armchairs. These fully-upholstered chairs are covered in a light cream fabric which accentuates the dark wood of the arms and legs.

"*W*all treatment was kept neutral and unadorned except for a 'presentation cabinet' opposite the windows. This cabinetry houses modern presentation equipment for use with slides and videos, and features a storage space which affords quick access to supplies and brochures as needed. The uncluttered, tasteful design of this boardroom creates an efficient distraction-free environment suitable to the scope and intensity of the business to be conducted within its walls."

Gaby Widajanti, HDII, IAI, Ahara Prima Design Pt. Interior Design
Jl. Birah II No. 4, Kebayoran Baru, Jakarta 12120, Indonesia
Tel.: (62) 21-712-388, (62) 21-720-7432, Fax: (62) 21-720-7432

Evan Williams

*B*oth an architect and interior designer, Evan Williams brings varied, impressive credentials to his numerous commercial, residential, hotel and restaurant design projects. Born in Kingston, Jamaica, Mr. Williams attended Pratt Institute in New York, and his Bachelors Degree in Architecture helped prepare him for his highly successful career throughout the Caribbean. His expertise has merited high accolades from his peers, and he has received several distinguished awards including the Governor General's Award for Excellence in Architecture presented by the Jamaica Institute of Architects as well as the Silver Musgrave Centenary Medal, Jamaica 21 Award for Excellence in Architecture. Mr. Williams presently owns an architectural firm and an interior design firm, based in Kingston, with associated offices in London, New York, Bogota, Barbados, Trinidad and St. Lucia.

"*I* wanted the natural feeling of my native Jamaica to greet the guests of the Grand Lido Hotel when they entered the main lobby and reception area. Visitors should be able to enjoy the perceptions of light, openness and natural simplicity, and still appreciate the sophisitication and elegance of this world-class hotel. The focal point of the soaring, octagonal ceiling is the chandelier which I designed and had manufactured in Florence. It is suspended beneath a traditional West Indian Georgian ceiling of timber. This roof is separated from a reinforced concrete ring beam by a continuous band of glazing.

"*H*igh paneled windows provide an abundance of natural light during the day, and the dentil molding on the face of the concrete beams conceals the perimeter lighting which warmly illuminates the lobby at night. Native limestone in shades of pink and beige cover the floors, walls and columns of the lobby. The effect, enhanced by the frequent use of plants and floral arrangements, creates an intimate grandeur that is both inviting and stately.

"*T*he room is sparsely furnished with Biedermier-style seating and *faux* stone pedestal tables in accent colors of orange and black. The carvings and decorations on the center pedestals represent the rams' heads and fertility symbols common to native religious beliefs. The open, arched entry into the main reception area provides a continuum of movement between the two areas for the guests as they get their first or final chance to appreciate the beauty of the hotel."

Evan Michael Williams, DCI International Interior Designers
19 Surbiton Road, Kingston 10, Jamaica
Tel.: (809) 926-4288, Fax: (809) 929-2007

Photography: Masato Yahagi

220

Ayako Yahagi

*B*orn in Sapporo City, Hokkaido, Japan, Ayako Yahagi received a Bachelor of Architecture degree from the Nihon University in Tokyo in 1966. A Certified First Class Architect, she established A & 3M Environmental Planning in 1972. Her major projects include numerous shopping centers, office buildings, and multi-unit and single-family residences. Ayako Yahagi is also a lecturer, planner and participant in various design-related seminars.

"*M*y challenge in designing the main office lobby for SRA, an international software company, was to integrate the high-tech world of computers into the traditional Japanese culture of stone gardens, bamboo, wood and paper. In the woodwork, I allowed the natural form and grain of zelkova trees to prevail as key design elements. The wood's golden glow permits the louvered ceiling to warm and counterpoint the stark, pale-toned walls, as do the green baseboards. Potted plants and organic shapes – the back of the throne-like, two-seat chair and the long wooden slab emblazoned with the corporate logo – let nature indoors. The boomerang-shaped wall sculpture, somewhat resembling seagulls in flight, is echoed by the form of the table across the room.

"*I* laid the carpet, a checkerboard pattern in natural green tones, on the diagonal to increase the sense of spaciousness and to undercut geometricality. The display in the stone garden, to the right of the chair, is changed with the seasons. As seen here for a New Year's presentation, tall stalks of bamboo are wrapped with paper sashes recalling kimono belts – another bow to tradition. On the wall behind them, shuttlecock-shaped decorations add a delicate touch of color. The seated doll, which is the company mascot, adds a bit of intimacy to a setting where traditional materials combine in a modern setting. As the indirect light passes through the wooden zelkova louvres, the room expresses a moment of stillness waiting for a new spring."

Ayako Yahagi, A&3M Environment Planning Company
5-29-7-302 Sendagaya, Shibuya-ku, Tokyo 151, Japan
Tel.: (81) 3-3358-4268, Fax: (81) 3-3226-7859

New York Branch:
128 West 13th Street, Suite 19, New York, New York 10011
Tel.: (212) 989-6374, Fax: (212) 989-8199

Jaci Yoap, IFDA

*J*aci Yoap specializes in Asian designs, particularly Chinese. In addition to interior design, she is also the designer of her own line of furnishings, and travels internationally for both the manufacture and marketing of her exclusive lines. Jaci Yoap has over twenty years of interior design experience, and lectures on Chinese arts, history, and the culture of the Chinese people.

"*M*y goal was to bring together all of the different collections on display in my design showroom. I employed a mixture of harmonious woods to create a warmth and elegance in this spacious area. Most of the furnishings are my own exclusive designs or antique pieces which I found on various trips and had refurbished by Ideal Antiques of Michigan. Because my *metier* is the ecletic blending of Asian, European and Victorian American antiques and special designs, I wanted this room to be an eloquent showcase of my design specialty."

Jaci Yoap, Interiors by Jaci
Highway B, Pound, Wisconsin 54161
Tel.: (414) 897-3536, Fax: (414) 897-2825

Photography: Val Ihde

223

fin.

Indexes . . .

Indexes

Designers Index: Whether for a private residence or for a commercial project, selecting the right interior designer is rarely an easy choice. To assist you with your decision, this book has been specially edited to act as a portfolio illustrating the finest work of a wide range of the world's leading interior designers.

On the preceding pages, you have had the opportunity to see each designer and to learn about their backgrounds and qualifications. You have been able to see their favorite design projects and read each designer's explanation of how they rose to the challenges each project presented. If this book has been successful, you probably have at least one designer in mind to interview for your upcoming interior design project. After selecting a designer offering the right style, the right look, and the right design philosophy, the next question usually concerns fees and payment structures.

On the following pages, each of the participating designers has provided contact information, a listing of their design specializations, and a general idea of their design fees. Almost all of the designers featured in this edition work internationally, and all have agreed to provide immediate attention to inquiries from readers of this book. You probably already know which of these one hundred designers is the best for you – and all it takes now is a simple phone call to make *your* design project that designer's new favorite!

Photographers Index: For the professional designer or architect, this book doubles as an international portfolio of the world's best interior and architectural photographers. The preceding pages have featured the finest examples of their work, and you are now invited to use the following index to locate and contact these professionals for projects throughout the world. Each index listing includes the photographer's name, company, address, telephone and fax numbers, as well as the pages on which their work appears. Whether your projects are in North America, Asia, South America, Europe or the Middle East, this index is a convenient contact directory of qualified interior and architectural photographers virtually anywhere in the world.

Designers Index

Jack Adams, ASID
Adams Design, Inc.
1415 Kalakaua Avenue, Suite 204
Honolulu, Hawaii 96826
Tel.: (808) 955-6100, Fax: (808) 947-4311
Residential, hotel and restaurant interior
design.
Fee structure: available upon request.
Pages 82-83

Roberto Alcantara
Spacio Planeacion y Diseno SA de CV
Lira #33, Col. Prados de Coyoacan
Mexico City CP 04810 DF, Mexico
Tel.: (52) 5-679-9813, Fax: (52) 5-679-9813
Residential, office and restaurant interior
design.
Fee structure: no consultation fee, fee for draft
and project, percentage of cost.
Pages 158-159

Sinee Amoradhat
Design 103 Ltd.
9/F, Asoke Towers Office Building
219 Asoke Road
Bangkok 10110, Thailand
Tel.: (66) 2-260-0160, Fax: (66) 2-259-1191
Residential, office, factory, educational, hotel
and restaurant interior design.
Fee structure: available upon request.
Pages 160-161

Michael Anthony
Michael Anthony Associates
Sixty-Six Eureka Street
San Francisco, California 94114
Tel.: (415) 255-3066, Fax: (415) 255-9168
Residential, contract and office interior design.
Fee structure: varies according to project.
Pages 84-85

Anthony Antine, ISID
Antine Associates
1028 Arcadian Way
Palisade, New Jersey 07024
Tel.: (201) 224-0315
Residential, contract and hotel interior design.
Fee structure: available upon request.
Pages 18-19

Countess Monika Apponyi, MCSD, IDDA, FISID
MM Design London
16 South Terrace
London, SW7 England
Tel.: (44) 71-584-7267, Fax: (44) 71-823-8288
Residential, contract, hotel and restaurant
interior design.
Fee structure: available upon request.
Pages 124-125

Katherine Bacon, NBSD
The Finishing Touch, Inc.
101-105 Charlotte Street
St. John, New Brunswick, Canada E2L 2J2
Tel.: (506) 633-1358, Fax: (506) 632-4064
Residential, contract and funeral home interior
design.
Fee structure: hourly fee.
Pages 162-163

Douglas Bartoli
Bartoli Interior Design
408 Plaza Rubio
Santa Barbara, California 93103
Tel.: (805) 569-9212, Fax: (805) 569-9214
Residential, contract, office, hotel and
restaurant interior design.
Fee structure: available upon request.
Pages 86-87

Ernesto Francisco Bedmar
Bedmar & Shi Designers Pte., Ltd.
11 Dhoby Ghaut #08-09, Cathay Building
Singapore 0922
Tel.: (65) 336-5022, Fax: (65) 339-0010
Office, museum, hotel and restaurant interior
design; restoration.
Fee structure: hourly fee or 10% of total
contract value, or lump sum figure (whichever
is higher).
Pages 164-165

Cristina Bertolazzi
Piani & Disegni Arquitetura e Interiores
Rua da Consolacao, 3407 Casa 6
Sao Paulo SP, Brazil 01416001
Tel.: (55) 11-280-7011, Fax: (55) 11-280-7578
Residential and office interior design.
Fee structure: available upon request.
Pages 126-127

Charles J. Bommarito, ASID
National Interiors
19380 Ten Mile Road
Eastpointe, Michigan 48021
Tel.: (313) 771-2260, Fax: (313) 771-2927
Residential interior design.
Fee structure: available upon request.
Pages 20-21

Consuelo Boom
Muebleria Frey
Periferico Sur 5128, Pedregal de Carrasco
Mexico DF, Mexico 04700
Tel.: (52) 5-665-6566, Fax: (52) 5-666-1668
Showroom, contract and residential interior
design.
Fee structure: available upon request.
Pages 166-167

Janet Bourne
Janet Bourne Interiors
3221 Lakewood Road
Glen Allen, Virginia 23060
Tel.: (800) 682-1251
Residential and contract interior design.
Fee structure: varies according to project.
Pages 22-23

Gloria Bordaberry Boxer
Interior Designer
Ing. Luis Andreoni 7210
Carrasco-Montevideo, Uruguay
Tel.: (598) 2-60-17-02, Fax: (598) 2-60-35-40
Residential and office interior design.
Fee structure: available upon request.
Pages 128-129

Diane Waltzek Boyer, ASID
Boyer-Cooper Interiors, Ltd.
32 Godwin Avenue
Midland Park, New Jersey 07432
Tel.: (201) 445-8412, Fax: (201) 445-2987
Residential, office, contract, hotel and
restaurant interior design.
Fee structure: varies according to project.
Pages 24-25

Carol Donayre Bugg, ASID
Decorating Den
7910 Woodmont Avenue
Bethesda, Maryland 20814
Tel.: (800) 428-1366, (301) 652-6393
Fax: (301) 652-9017
Residential interior design.
Fee structure: no consultation fee.
Pages 26-27

Moon-Young Choi
Kofuco Interiors Co., Ltd.
957 Konghang-Dong, Kangshu-Ku
Seoul, South Korea
Tel.: (82) 2-665-1141, Fax: (82) 2-661-1141
Residential and contract interior architecture
and design.
Fee structure: varies according to project.
Pages 168-69

Ann Cooper
Boyer-Cooper Interiors, Ltd.
32 Godwin Avenue
Midland Park, New Jersey 07432
Tel.: (201) 445-8412, Fax: (201) 445-2987
Residential, office, contract, hotel and
restaurant interior design.
Fee structure: varies according to project.
Pages 28-29

Cordelia Cortes
Cordelia Cortes, S.A.
Cerrada de Tecamachalco 114
11560 Mexico DF, Mexico
Tel.: (52) 5-520-5078, Fax: (52) 5-202-7325
Residential, office, hotel and restaurant interior
design.
Fee structure: varies according to project.
Pages 88-89

Martha O. Dalitzky, ASID
Studio East Inc.
15 Benton Drive, Post Office Box 487
East Longmeadow, Massachusetts 01028
Tel.: (413) 525-4850, Fax: (413) 567-8971
Residential, contract, office and model home
interior design.
Fee structure: varies depending on size and
scope of project.
Pages 30-31

Michael de Santis, ASID
Michael de Santis, Inc.
1110 Second Avenue at 58th Street
New York, New York 10022
Tel.: (212) 753-8871, Fax: (212) 935-7777
Residential interior design.
Fee structure: available upon request.
Pages 4, 16-17, 32-33, lower left back cover

Susan Ley Dearborn
Solutions by Susan Ley Dearborn
30 Cliff Road
Wellesley, Massachusetts 02181
Tel.: (617) 235-2920
Residential and office interior design.
Fee structure: determined by size and scale of
project.
Pages 34-35

Suellen DeFrancis
Suellen DeFrancis Architectural Interiors, Inc.
Post Office Box 247
Scarsdale, New York 10583
Tel.: (914) 472-8013, Fax: (914) 472-5235
Residential, office, hotel and restaurant interior design.
Fee structure: hourly fee, plus percentage of net purchases.
Pages 36-37

Iris DeMauro
Iris DeMauro, Inc.
115 Mercer Street
New York, New York 10012
Tel.: (212) 226-7766, Fax: (212) 529-5654
Residential, contract, hotel and restaurant interior design.
Fee structure: available upon request.
Pages 38-39

Robert Dirstein
Dirstein Robertson Limited
77 Yorkville Avenue
Toronto, Ontario, Canada M5R 1C1
Tel.: (416) 961-6211, Fax: (416) 961-5537
Residential interior design.
Fee structure: available upon request.
Pages 40-41

Rodger Dobbel, ASID
Rodger Dobbel Interiors
23 Vista Avenue
Piedmont, California 94611
Tel.: (510) 654-6723, Fax: (510) 658-7556
Residential interior design.
Fee structure: available upon request.
Pages 90-91

Trudy Dujardin, ASID
Trudy Dujardin Interiors
Post Office Box 2655 Saugatuck Station
3 Sylvan Road South
Westport, Connecticut 06880
Tel.: (203) 222-1019
Residential interior design.
Fee structure: available upon request.
Pages 42-43

Beverly Ellsley
Beverly Ellsley, Inc.
175 Post Road
Westport, Connecticut 06880
Tel.: (203) 227-1157, Fax: (203) 227-6681
Residential interior design; kitchens and custom cabinetry.
Fee structure: varies according to project.
Pages 44-45

William R. Eubanks
William R. Eubanks Interior Design
1516 Union Avenue
Memphis, Tennessee 38104
Tel.: (901) 272-1825, Fax: (901) 272-1845
Residential and contract interior design.
Fee structure: available upon request.
Pages 46-47

John Ford, FASID
John Ford Associates, Inc.
2601 North Charles Street
Baltimore, Maryland 21218
Tel.: (410) 467-9400, Fax: (410) 243-3451
Residential interior design; art specialist.
Fee structure: available upon request.
Pages 48-49

Arlene Golub, ASID
Arlene Golub Interiors
6409 Tilden Lane
Rockville, Maryland 20852
Tel.: (301) 881-6008, Fax: (301) 881-6008
Residential and contract interior design.
Fee structure: hourly fee, plus percentage of net purchases; varies according to project.
Pages 50-51

Vicki Grace, FCSD
Addison Marc (M) Sdn Bhd
7 Jalan Kia Peng
Kuala Lumpur 50450, Malaysia
Tel.: (60) 3-248-2416, Fax: (60) 3-248-2164
Contract and residential interior design.
Fee structure: varies according to project.
Pages 130-131

Lisbeth Mathisen Grundt
Design Concept
Uranienborg Terr. 10
Oslo, Norway 0351
Tel.: (47) 22-46-56-23, Fax: (47) 22-64-03-04
Residential, office and contract interior design.
Fee structure: hourly fee, plus percentage of net purchases.
Pages 132-133

Solichin Gunawan, HDII
P.T. Atelier 6 Interior
Jalan Cikini IV/20-A
Jakarta, Indonesia 10330
Tel: (62) 21-310-0276, Fax: (62) 21-310-3396
Hotel and restaurant interior design.
Fee structure: available upon request.
Pages 170-171

Mark Hampton, ASID
Mark Hampton, Inc.
654 Madison Avenue
New York, New York 10021
Tel.: (212) 753-4110, Fax: (212) 758-2079
Residential and contract interior design.
Fee structure: available upon request.
Pages 52-53

Allison Holland, ASID
Creative Decorating
168 Poloke Place
Honolulu, Hawaii 96822
Tel.: (808) 955-1465, Fax: (808) 949-2290
Residential interior design; unusual creative projects.
Fee structure: available upon request; depends upon volume and type of project.
Pages 92-93

Joseph P. Horan, ASID
Joseph Horan Interior Design
3299 Washington Street
San Francisco, California 94115
Tel.: (415) 346-5646
Residential interior design.
Fee structure: available upon request.
Front flyleaf, pages 1, 13, 94-95

Charles "Chip" A. Johnston, Jr., ASID, IFDA
Chip Johnston Interiors
2996 Grandview Avenue, N.E., Suite 300
Atlanta, Georgia 30305
Tel.: (404) 231-4141
Residential interior design.
Fee structure: available upon request.
Pages 54-55

Leonardo Junqueira
Piani & Disegni Arquitetura e Interiores
Rua da Consolacao, 3407 Casa 6
Sao Paulo SP, Brazil 01416001
Tel.: (55) 11-280-7011, Fax: (55) 11-280-7578
Residential and office interior design.
Fee structure: varies according to project.
Pages 134-135

Masae Kawamura
Kanko Kikaku Sekkeisha,
Yozo Shibata & Associates
No. 9 Mori Building, 1-2-3 Atago
Minato-ku, Tokyo 105, Japan
Tel.: (81) 3-3434-4674, Fax: (81) 3-3434-2297
Hotel and restaurant interior design.
Fee structure: available upon request.
Pages 172-173

Adrienne Kamp, ISID
K & R Interiors, Ltd.
6858 North Latrobe
Skokie, Illinois 60077
Tel.: (708) 674-6858, Fax: (708) 673-2634
Residential interior design.
Fee structure: available upon request.
Pages 56-57

Dale Keller
Dale Keller Associates, Ltd.
1501 Stanhope House, 738 King's Road
North Point, Hong Kong
Tel.: (852) 565-6255, Fax: (852) 565-9494
Hotel and restaurant interior design.
Fee structure: available upon request.
Pages 174-175

Tessa Kennedy, ISID
Tessa Kennedy Designs, Limited
Studio 5, 97 Freston Road
London W11 4BD, England
Tel.: (44) 71-22-4546, Fax: (44) 71-229-2899

314 North Foothill
Beverly Hills, California 90210
Tel.: (310) 273-4097, Fax: (310) 273-9948
Residential, office, yacht, hotel and restaurant interior design.
Fee structure: available upon request.
Pages 176-177

Rebecca Key
Alexander Key and Associates
2129 Maryland Avenue
Baltimore, Maryland 21218
Tel.: (410) 962-5365, Fax: (410) 962-7324
Retail, contract, nursing home and retirement center interior design.
Fee structure: varies according to project.
Pages 178-179

Norma King
Norma King Designz
P.O. Box 980172
Houston, Texas 77098
Tel.: (713) 524-1172

P.O. Box 70043, Glyfada
16610 Athens, Greece
Tel.: (30) 1-984-2039
Residential, hotel and casino interior design.
Fee structure: varies according to project.
Pages 96-97

Patricia Klee
PK Design
Post Office Box 31150
Santa Barbara, California 93130
Tel.: (805) 687-7894, Fax: (805) 969-0390
Residential, office, hotel and restaurant interior design; design for agri-business complexes and ranches.
Fee structure: available upon request.
Pages 98-99

Richard H. Klein, BSID
Hamma Galleries
One Lane Hill
Hamilton 5, Bermuda
Tel: (809) 292-8500, Fax: (809) 292-8424
Residential interior design.
Fee structure: available upon request.
Pages 136-137

Nancy Kwok, MCSD
Hinex Universal Design Contracting Co., Ltd.
4501 China Resources Building
26 Harbour Road
Wanchai, Hong Kong
Tel.: (852) 827-8077, Fax: (852) 827-7917
Contract, office, hotel and restaurant interior design.
Fee structure: varies according to project.
Pages 180-181

Pat Larin, ASID
Pat Larin Interiors
12720 Dianne Drive
Los Altos Hills, California 94022
Tel.: (415) 941-4613, Fax: (415) 941-4047
Residential, office, restaurant and small hotel interior design; remodelling projects; new construction.
Fee structure: varies according to project.
Pages 100-101

Ricardo Lazo
Ricardo Lazo Textiles
Insurgentes Sur 2047-C
San Angel DF CP 01000, Mexico
Tel: (52) 5-661-1197, (52) 5-661-9196
Fax: (52) 5-661-9196
Residential interior design (others, depending upon project); fabric design.
Fee structure: varies according to project.
Pages 182-183

Cynthia Leftwich, ASID, IBD
Leftwich & Associates
1711 Avenue J, Suite 108
Lubbock, Texas 79401
Tel.: (806) 747-5584, Fax: (806) 762-2044
Contract and office interior design.
Fee structure: varies according to project.
Pages 14, 184-185

Barbara LeVin
Barbara LeVin Interiors
120 East 56th Street, Suite 515
New York, New York, 10022
Tel.: (212) 688-9070, Fax: (212) 688-9069
Residential and office interior design.
Fee structure: available upon request.
Pages 58-59

Makoto Maehara
Maehara Makoto Design Room
1-25-5 Yutenji, Meguro-ku
Tokyo 153, Japan
Tel.: (81) 3-3710-0736, Fax: (81) 3-3710-0736
Residential, office, hotel and restaurant interior design; furniture and art object design.
Fee structure: percentage of net purchases or hourly fee if required.
Pages 186-187

Rod Maxwell, ISID
R.A. Maxwell, Inc.
5461 N. East River Road, Suite 901
Chicago, Illinois 60656
Tel.: (312) 693-2857, Fax: (312) 693-6620
Residential interior design.
Fee structure: available upon request.
Pages 60-61

Ricardo Mayer, ASID
Arquitetura e Palnejamento
680-708 Avenida Copoacabana
Rio de Janeiro, Brazil 22050
Tel.: (54) 21-256-8616, Fax: (54) 21-256-8616
Residential, hotel and restaurant interior design.
Fee structure: varies according to project.
Pages 5, 138-139

H. Glenn McGee, AIA, ASID
McGee-Howle & Associates, Architects, Inc.
2801 Ocean Drive, Suite 302
Vero Beach, Florida 32963
Tel.: (407) 231-4222, Fax: (407) 231-4311
Residential interior design.
Fee structure: varies according to project.
Pages 62-63

Carol Meltzer, ASID
P.T.M. Interiors
51 East 82nd Street
New York, New York 10028
Tel.: (212) 737-5139, Fax: (212) 737-5139

64345 Via Risso
Palm Springs, California 92262
Tel.: (619) 322-0702, Fax: (619) 322-6084
Residential, office, boutique, hotel and restaurant interior design.
Fee structure: available upon request.
Pages 64-65, 80-81

Anthony Michael
Interior Design, Ltd.
844 West Erie
Chicago, Illinois 60622
Tel.: (312) 243-2430, Fax: (312) 243-3651
Residential, hotel and restaurant interior design.
Fee structure: design fee based on project and cost plus 35% of purchases.
Pages 82-83

Yoshiko Mononobe
AIAP Interior Design
3-11-8-1206 Setagaya, Setagaya-ku
Tokyo, Japan
Tel.: (81) 3-3426-5057, Fax: (81) 3-5450-1275
Residential, office, gallery and hotel interior design.
Fee structure: available upon request.
Pages 140-141

Cheryl Monroe, ASID
Monroe & Company International, Inc.
555 108th Northeast, Suite 1
Bellevue, Washington 98004
Tel.: (206) 455-3227, Fax: (206) 455-4098
Residential, office, hotel and restaurant interior design.
Fee structure: varies according to project, available upon request.
Pages 102-103

Vinicio Montalvo
ACM & M Arquitectos Asociados
Callao 3227, Las Condes
Santiago, Chile
Tel.: (56) 2-233-3088, Fax: (56) 2-233-1989
Residential, office, hotel and restaurant design.
Fee structure: varies according to project.
Pages 188-189

Kevin Patrick Mullarkey, MIDDA
Cotton Box Interiors
21 Middle Street
Galway, Ireland
Tel: (353) 91-64373, Fax: (353) 91-64383
Residential, hotel and restaurant interior design.
Fee structure: fixed fee for each project.
Pages 142-143

Wajih Naccache
Design Team
Naser Street, Post Office Box 1776
Sharjah, United Arab Emirates
Tel.: (971) 6-593-035, Fax.: (971) 6-597-521
Tlx.: 68230 EM
Residential interior design.
Fee structure: varies according to project.
Pages 122-123, 144-145

Seiichi Nakagawa, JID
MHS Planners, Architects & Engineers
1-5-17, Moto Akasaka, Minato-ku
Tokyo 107, Japan
Tel.: (81) 3-3403-6161, Fax: (81) 3-3404-6515
Office, hotel, restaurant, club and resort interior design.
Fee structure: varies according to project.
Pages 156-157, 190-191, lower right back cover

Prem Nath, ASID
Prem Nath & Associates
4, Merewether Road, Apollo Bunder
Bombay 400 039, India
Tel.: (91) 22-202-0029, Fax: (91) 22-287-5150
Residential, office, hotel and restaurant interior design.
Fee structure: percentage of overall cost, varies according to project.
Pages 146-147

Walter Nelson, ASID
Nelson Limited
Post Office Box 4130
Leucadia, California 92023
Tel.: (619) 753-9058, Fax: (619) 753-3787
Residential, office, hotel and restaurant interior design.
Fee structure: available upon request.
Pages 10-11, 104-105

Sandra Nunnerley, ASID
Sandra Nunnerley, Inc.
112 East 71st Street, Suite 3B
New York, New York 10021
Tel: (212) 472-9341, Fax: (212) 472-9346
Residential, and specialized office and retail showroom interior design.
Fee structure: available upon request.
Pages 2, 6-7, 68-69

Joshua Jih Pan, AIA
J.J. Pan & Partners
21, Alley 12, Lane 118, Ren Ai Road, Sec. 3
Taipei, Taiwan, ROC
Tel.: (886) 2-701-2617, Fax: (886) 2-700-4489
Residential, educational, high-tech industrial and commercial interior architecture and design.
Fee structure: available upon request.
Pages 192-193

Penni Paul
Penni Paul Interiors
170 South Beverly Drive
Beverly Hills, California 90212
Tel.: (310) 276-8005, Fax: (310) 276-8908
Residential, contract, office, hotel, restaurant
and religious structure interior design.
Fee structure: available upon request.
Pages 106-107

Alberto Pinto
Cabinet Alberto Pinto
61 Quai d'Orsay
Paris 75007, France
Tel.: (33) 1-45-51-03-33
Fax: (33) 1-45-55-51-41
Residential, office, private yacht, hotel, resort
and restaurant interior design.
Pages 148-149, upper-right back cover

Carlos A. Profet
INARCH
Vondellaan 19-B
Oranjestad, Aruba
Tel.: (297) 8-25677, Fax: (297) 8-32574
Office, contract and residential interior design.
Fee structure: varies according to project.
Pages 194-195

German Quiroga
Intermobel Office Furniture, SA de CV
Ave. Torres de Ixtapantongo #380
Col. Olivar los Padres
Mexico City DF, Mexico 01780
Tel.: (52) 5-595-8667, Fax: (52) 5-595-1589
Convention/exposition center, theatre and
contract interior design.
Fee structure: varies according to project.
Pages 196-197

Gerd Ramstad
Gerd Ramstad Interiorarkitekt Nil
Lovenskioldsvei 16-B
1342 Jar, Norway
Tel.: (47) 2-53-04-58, Fax: (47) 2-12-34-10
Contract, office, hotel and restaurant interior
design.
Fee structure: available upon request.
Pages 198-199

Leticia Chaves Ray
Leticia Ray Interior Design
Mariscal Estigarribia 1636
Asuncion, Paraguay
Tel.: (595) 21-200-612, Fax: (595) 21-210-846
Residential, office and restaurant interior
design.
Fee structure: varies according to project.
Pages 150-151

Jenny Real-Ortiz
Telas, Ideas y Proyectos, SA de CV
Monte Libano 255, Lamos de Chapultepec
Mexico City DF, Mexico 11000
Tel.: (52) 5-540-2053, Fax: (52) 5-202-6170
Residential and contract interior design.
Fee structure: available upon request.
Pages 108-109

Gloria Roberts, ISID
Gloria Balogh Interiors
1733 Massachusetts Avenue
Riverside, California 92507
Tel.: (909) 787-9279, Fax: (909) 683-7291
Residential, office and educational interior
design.
Fee structure: available upon request.
Pages 110-111

Judy Robins
Judy Robins Interiors
755 Lafayette Street
Denver, Colorado 80218
Tel.: (303) 832-3265, Fax: (303) 830-6939
Residential interior design.
Fee structure: varies according to project.
Pages 112-113

Gwen Pardun Rotolo, ISID
Interiors by Gwen
43 W. Robertson
Palatine, Illinois 60067
Tel.: (800) 354-GWEN (354-4936)

10115 E. Mt. View Road, Suite 1101
Scottsdale, Arizona 85858
Tel.: (602) 661-1952, Fax: (602) 661-1952
Residential and contract interior design.
Fee structure: available upon request.
Pages 70-71

Darryl Savage
DHS Designs
5530 Wisconsin Avenue, Suite 1610
Chevy Chase, Maryland 20815
Tel.: (301) 858-6391, Fax: (301) 913-2037
Residential, hotel and restaurant design.
Fee structure: design retainer plus percentage
of net purchases.
Pages 72-73

Petra Schleifenheimer
Innenarchitecktin
Fuerther Strasse 91a
8500 Nuremberg 80, Germany
Tel.: (49) 911-289042, Fax: (49) 911-284641
Residential, office, hotel and restaurant interior
design.
Fee structure: varies according to project,
available upon request.
Pages 200-201

Der Scutt, FAIA
Der Scutt Architect
44 West 28th Street
New York, New York 10001
Tel.: (212) 725-2300, Fax: (212) 481-7094
Office and commercial architectural/interior
design.
Fee structure: available upon request.
Pages 8-9, 12, 202-203

Rohini Shanker
Consultant on Interior Design
#15, 2nd Avenue, Harrington Road
Madras, India 600-031
Tel.: (91) 44-860-970, Fax: (91) 44-860-970
Office, contract and residential interior design.
Fee structure: available upon request.
Pages 204-205

Yozo Shibata
Kanko Kikaku Sekkeisha,
Yozo Shibata & Associates
No. 9 Mori Building, 1-2-3 Atago
Minato-ku, Tokyo 105, Japan
Tel.: (81) 3-3434-4674, Fax: (81) 3-3434-2297
Hotel and restaurant interior design.
Fee structure: available upon request.
Pages 206-207

Mary Sorenson
Cedar Hill Design Center, Inc.
712 Cedar Street
Cedar Hill, Texas 75104
Tel.: (214) 291-2070, Fax: (214) 293-0378
Residential and office interior design.
Fee structure: varies according to project.
Pages 114-115

Maureen Sullivan Stemberg
Maureen Sullivan Stemberg Interior Design
211 Berkley Street
Boston, Massachusetts 02116
Tel: (617) 536-8464, Fax: (617) 536-1750
Palm Beach: Tel: (407) 659-7126
Residential, hotel and restaurant interior
design.
Fee structure: hourly fee, plus percentage of
net purchases.
Front cover, pages 74-75, 224

Chatchawal Submuang
Design 103 Ltd.
9/F, Asoke Towers Ofc. Bldg., 219 Asoke Rd.
Bangkok 10110, Thailand
Tel.: (66) 2-260-0160, Fax: (66) 2-259-1191
Residential, office, factory, educational, hotel
and restaurant interior design.
Fee structure: available upon request.
Pages 208-209

David I. Tay
David Tay & Associates
10 Anson Road, #30-16 International Plaza
Singapore 0207
Tel.: (65) 221-2716, Fax: (65) 224-8805
Residential, contract, hotel, restaurant and
museum interior design.
Fee structure: available upon request.
Pages 210-211

Jacqueline Thwaites, ISID
Inchbald School of Design
32 Eccleston Square
London, England SW1V 1PB
Tel.: (44) 71-630-9011, Fax: (44) 71-976-5979
Residential and contract interior design.
Fee structure: available upon request.
Pages 152-153

Victor Tom, ASID, CSID
Design Group A
288 Kuang Fu South Road, 4th Floor, Suite 5
Taipei, Taiwan, ROC
Tel.: (886) 2-776-5506, Fax: (886) 2-731-5620
Office, hotel and restaurant interior design.
Fee structure: varies according to project.
Pages 212-213

Jacob Tsang
Suika Interior Design, Inc.
50 Weybright Court, Unit 13
Scarborough, Ontario, M1S 5A8, Canada
Tel.: (416) 609-3668, (416) 258-6708
Fax: (416) 609-9998
Residential, contract, hotel and restaurant
interior design.
Fee structure: available upon request.
Pages 214-215

Edward Turrentine, ASID
Edward C. Turrentine Interior Design, Inc.
70 North Raymond Avenue
Pasadena, California 91103
Tel.: (818) 795-9964, Fax: (818) 795-0027
Residential and contract interior design.
Fee structure: available upon request.
Pages 3, 116-117

Lee Walsh
Lee Walsh Interiors/Interiors By Design
Post Office Box 64590
Unionville, Ontario, Canada L3R 0M9
Tel.: (416) 470-6122, Fax: (416) 470-7448
Residential and commercial interior design;
customized furniture design.
Fee structure: available upon request.
Pages 76-77

Photographers Index

Tina Freeman
The Decatur Studio, Inc.
1090 Magazine Street
New Orleans, Louisiana
Tel.: (504) 523-3000, Fax: (504) 581-4397
Pages 46-47

Bernardo Fuchs
Bernardo Fuchs Fotografia
Dr. Vertiz #736-102 Col. Narvarte
Mexico City DF, Mexico
Pages 158-159

Weston Gorin
Gorin Photography
1138 20th Street, Suite 6
Santa Monica, California 90403
Tel.: (310) 453-3339
Pages 106-107

Kevin Gorman
Specialized Photography
Post Office Box 3188
Vero Beach, FL 32963
Tel.: (407) 231-6109
Pages 62-63

Anne Gummerson
Anne Gummerson Photography
811 South Ann Street
Baltimore, Maryland 21231
Tel.: (410) 732-4429, (410) 235-8325
Fax: (410) 467-2503
Pages 22-23, 72-73

Steve Hall
Hedrich-Blessing
11 West Illinois Street
Chicago, Illinois 60610
Tel.: (312) 321-1151, Fax: (312) 321-1165
Pages 70-71

Seow Cheong Heng
Xiao Photo Workshop
Block 104, #02-232 Geylang East Avenue 3
Singapore 1438
Tel.: (65) 743-4831, Fax: (65) 704-0252
Pages 164-165

Douglas Hill
Los Angeles, California
Page 3

Val Ihde
Val Ihde Photographers
805 Sixth Avenue
Menominee, Michigan 49858
Tel.: (906) 864 2369
Pages 222-223

Luis Hernan Herreros Infante
ACM & M Arquitectos Asociados
Callao 3227, Las Condes
Santiago, Chile
Tel.: (56) 2-233-3088, Fax: (56) 2-233-1989
Pages 188-189

Linda Johnson
Linda Johnson Photography
2914 Huntingdon Avenue
Baltimore, Maryland 21211
Tel.: (410) 243-2117
Pages 178-179

Barbara Kagan
B.C. Kagan
43 Winter Street
Boston, Massachusetts 02108
Tel.: (617) 482-0336
Page 75

Paola Isola Kapitanakis
Paola Isola Photography
1203 Villmont
Houston, Texas 77024
Tel.: (713) 558-2969
Pages 96-97

Misso Kawakami
Tokyo, Japan
Pages 140-141

Sabine Ketzler
KL Foto-Studios Galerie
Rodergasse 11
8803 Rothenburg, Germany
Tel.: (49) 9861-7971
Pages 200-201

Jeff Kilpatrick
Pages 174-75

Gavin Kingcome
3-33 Shacklewell Street
London E2 7EG, England
Tel.: (44) 71-613-4432
Pages 124-125

Toshiharu Kitajima
Archi Photo Kitajima
3-704 Seto, Noda-shi
Chiba 278, Japan
Tel.: (81) 471-38-3247, Fax: (81) 471-38-3247
Pages 190-191

Jorge Köhli
Montevideo, Uruguay
Pages 128-129

James A. Langone
James A. Langone Photographer Inc.
36 Loring Street
Springfield, Massachusetts 01105
Tel.: (413) 732-1174, Fax: (413) 734-7698
Pages 30-31

Sigbjorn Lenes
Sigbjorn Lenes Reklamefoto A/S
Skolmar 13, Box 395
Sandefjord 3201, Norway
Tel.: (47) 34-76380, Fax: (47) 34-79140
Pages 198-199

James Levin
James Levin Studios
45 West 21st Street
New York, New York 10010
Tel.: (212) 242-5337, Fax: (212) 255-5914
Pages 64-65, 80-81

David Livingston
487 Greenwich Street
San Francisco, California 94133
Tel.: (415) 392-2465. Fax: (415) 398-3312
Pages 90-91, 92-93

Fernando Rafael Luidens
Check Point Color N.V.
Columbusstraat #10
Oranjestad, Aruba
Tel.: (297) 8-22284, Fax: (297) 8-38424
Pages 194-195

Charles Maraia
Maraia Photography
236 West 27th Street #804
New York, New York 10001
Tel.: (212) 206-8156
Page 26

Hilman Maulani
Jakarta, Indonesia
Page 171

Peter Mauss
c/o Esto Photographic
222 Valley Place
Mamaroneck, New York 10543
Tel.: (914) 698-4060, Fax: (914) 698-1033
Pages 8-9

Norman McGrath
164 79th Street
New York, New York 10024
Tel.: (212) 799-6422, Fax: (212) 799-6442
Pages 36-37, 202-203

Jon Miller
Hedrich-Blessing
11 West Illinois Street
Chicago, Illinois 60610
Tel.: (312) 321-1151, Fax: (312) 321-1165
Pages 60-61

Koshi Miwa
Kokyo Miwa Architectural Photograph
Laboratory
144 Noborito, Tama-ku
Kawasaki-shi, Kanagawa 24, Japan
Tel.: (81) 44-911-4354, Fax: (81) 44-911-7267
Pages 156-157, lower right back cover

Daisy Mo
Toronto, Canada
Pages 214-215

Juca Moraes
Rua Francisco Otaviano 60, Apto. 112
Copacabana CEP 22080, Brazil
Tel.: (55) 2-267-9735
Pages 5, 138-139, upper left back cover

Felipe Morales
New York, New York
Tel.: (212) 781-6835
Pages 38-39

James Mortimer
c/o World of Interiors
182 Stapleton Hall Road
London, England N4 4QL
Tel.: (44) 81-340-2545
Page 176

Michael Mundy
220 East 5th Street
New York, New York 10003
Tel.: (212) 529-7114
Page 2

Buzzy Muvsho
Pages 48-49

Daniel Nierman
Daniel Nierman Photographer
Reforma 16-B
San Angel 01000 DF, Mexico
Tel.: (52) 5-548-8433, Fax: (52) 5-548-8398
Pages 182-183

Peter Paige
269 Parkside Road
Harrington Park, New Jersey 07640
Tel.: (201) 767-3150, (212) 243-4935
Pages 18-19

In addition to the designers and photographers whom have participated in the publication of this book, special thanks is also offered to all those others whom provided valuable assistance in its creation: Don Burnett, M.A., Carla Copenhaven, Ph.D., and Janet Showalter (editorial); Jane Huang and Meaghan Maher (research); Kathryn Crabb, Richard Cromwell, Corinne Zink Kopen and Beth Robinson (production); the American Institute of Architects, the American Society of Interior Designers, the Institute of Business Designers, and the International Society of Interior Designers (text material). I would also like to thank Joseph P. Horan, Cynthia Leftwich, Ricardo Mayer, Carol Meltzer, Wajih Naccache, Seiichi Nakagawa, Walter Nelson, Sandra Nunnerley, Der Scutt, Maureen Sullivan Stemberg, Edward Turrentine, and Barbara Woolf for the photographs they provided for various introductory pages, and especially Michael de Santis both for the photographs he provided as well as for graciously taking the time to write the Foreword of this edition.

– J.L.P.

234